D0893342

The Archaeology of London
Series editors: John Schofield and Alan Vince

SAXON LONDON:

An Archaeological Investigation

Alan Vince

London

Typeset by Setrite Typesetters, Hong Kong
and printed and bound in Great Britain
by Biddles Ltd., Guildford, England
for the publishers
B.A. Seaby Ltd.
8, Cavendish Square
London W1M 0AJ

Distributed by
B.T. Batsford Ltd.
P.O. Box 4, Braintree, Essex CM7 7QY

ISBN 1 85264 019 7

British Library Cataloguing in Publication Data
Vince, Alan G. (Alan George, *1952−*)
Saxon London: an archaeological investigation.
(The Archaeology of London)
1. London. Antiquities. Archaeological ·investigation
I. Title II. Series
936.2′1

ISBN 1−85264−019−7

Contents

Acknowledgements

All the line illustrations used here are the work of Nick Griffiths, unless otherwise stated, and I would like to take this opportunity to thank him for them and for all the work he did for me at the Museum of London. The photographs are reproduced by permission of the Trustees of the Museum of London, except for Figures 6, 7, 30, 56 and 57 which are reproduced by permission of the Trustees of the British Museum. My text has been read in draft by Kate Steane and Chris Guy, both of the City of Lincoln Archaeological Unit. Without them the sentences would have been twice as tortuous.

The Museum of London employs two archaeological field units – the DUA and DGLA – whose combined staff since their formation must total several hundred. During the eight years I worked in the museum I was extremely lucky to be able to talk with many of the staff of these units, to see excavations and material as they were discovered and to discuss them with the archaeologists working on the recording and publication of the information. Whilst it is impossible to give credit to everyone whose work has helped me, I would like to place on record my thanks to Patrick Allen, Dave Bentley, Lyn Blackmore, Bob Cowie, Robin Densem, Geoff Egan, Charlotte Harding, Brian Hobley, Cathy Maloney, John Maloney, Louise Miller, Gustav Milne, Clive Orton, Dom Perring, Steve Roskams, Laura Schaaf, Derek Seeley, Harvey Sheldon, Bruce Watson and Rob Whytehead. Marion Archibald, John Clark, Catherine East, David Hinton, Frances Pritchard, Peter Stott, Leslie Webster and Sir David Wilson gave me advice on the date and significance of artefacts from Saxon London, while Jenny Hall and Hugh Chapman supplied me with information on late Roman finds, especially coins. The section on churches has benefited from being read by Richard Morris and David Stocker.

Many people have been kind enough to listen to my half-formed ideas over the years and have been patient enough to correct them whenever possible. First and foremost must be Tony Dyson who has put his time and his library at my disposal ever since I first came to London and who has read many drafts of papers on Saxon London for me. Both Derek Keene and John Clark have always been extremely helpful, full of ideas and generous with their time. I would like to thank John Schofield for suggesting that I write this book and for keeping me on my toes while I did it.

Introduction

The English language, many of our social institutions and most of our settlements have their origins in the Anglo-Saxon period and yet the material remains, with a few notable exceptions such as the Sutton Hoo ship burial, are insubstantial and unimpressive. It is no wonder, therefore, that books on Anglo-Saxon archaeology have tended to concentrate on written sources and decorative metalwork. Anglo-Saxon towns have had a bad press and it is still not uncommon to hear it said that the Anglo-Saxons had no use for towns, or that Alfred of Wessex and his successors introduced towns to England in the late ninth century. At present our views about the size and number of Anglo-Saxon towns which existed before Alfred are changing rapidly and one of the main reasons for this revision is the work which is in progress on Saxon London.

One of the main and surprising conclusions to have been reached is that London in the Saxon period, from some time in the fifth century until the Norman conquest, was not one settlement but two (see Fig. 1). For about two-thirds of the Saxon period, comprising three centuries, the main settlement lay outside the walls of the Roman city. In the second half of the ninth century the settlement moved within the walls but even then there are two quite distinct phases to be seen in the archaeological evidence. What is true for eleventh century London is not necessarily true for London in the late ninth or tenth centuries. It follows from this that there is no possibility of presenting a thematic survey of Saxon London without first setting out what is known of its historical development. In many cases this means that the same data are being used in different ways in different parts of this book. Nevertheless, it is hoped that in the end the reader is left with a clearer idea of what is actually known from contemporary evidence, what is inferred from later times and what is still surmise.

London is the capital city of the United Kingdom and from the fourteenth century at least (some would even claim by the twelfth) its development seems to diverge from that of other English towns. One of the possibilities of archaeological research in the Saxon period is to compare the London evidence with that from other towns, both in England and abroad. Here, possibly, we can see when Saxon London first showed signs of its later pre-eminence and to what extent the archaeology of Saxon London is also the archaeology of Saxon towns in general. The main sources of evidence

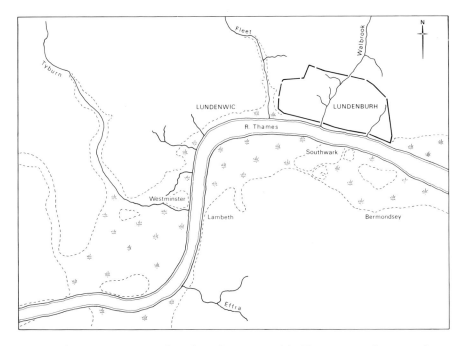

FIG. 1 The two Saxon towns of London. The position of the Thames cannot be accurately plotted and seems to have varied considerably during the Saxon period. It is possible to see the advantages of the two main crossing points – Southwark to *Lundenburh* and Lambeth to Westminster.

for Saxon London are: i) documents, ii) archaeological excavation, iii) the study of artefacts, iv) environmental archaeology, v) the study of coins, and vi) the study of place-names. These lines of research are not equally well studied at present and much of the source material remains unpublished. Indeed, in the case of archaeological excavation it is to be hoped that much remains to be excavated. Each type of source has different capabilities which are set out below.

Documentary evidence for Saxon London is sparse and, apart from Bede's *Ecclesiastical History of the English Nation* and the *Anglo-Saxon Chronicle*, mostly dates to the eleventh century. It consists of references in contemporary histories and chronicles, contemporary documents recording grants of land, collectively referred to as charters, and references to events or circumstances in Saxon London in later sources. It is important to realise that even contemporary records rarely survive in their original form and that errors and interpolations may have been added at any point before the writing of the earliest surviving text. Reliable translations of the contemporary records are available and have been commented upon and interpreted by generations of historians. For London the two most accessible works are Sir Frank Stenton's pamphlet entitled *Norman London*, and Christopher Brooke and Gillian Keir's *London 800–1216:*

The Shaping of a City. The latter was written at the very beginning of the current spate of archaeological work but little has been found since to alter the authors' conclusions about the social structure and institutions of later Saxon London. Indeed, in these two spheres at least it would take exceptional archaeological evidence to alter a conclusion based on contemporary documentary evidence. References to Saxon London in later documents have been used less by historians and ideally would be used only for what they show about the knowledge of the past by their writers and intended readership. Such documents may contain flights of fancy, such as those of Geoffrey of Monmouth, or may contain a grain of truth. Here there is more room for a collaboration between archaeologists and historians. In particular, statements about Offa's palace near St Alban Wood Street church, or the reason for the name of St Clement Danes may yet be proved or disproved by archaeology.

As with historical documents, so excavations are of varying value. First and foremost the evidence must survive to be recorded. On many sites in the city this is not the case. Terracing along the hillside leading down to the Thames has occasionally led to a build-up of deposits, preserving Saxon strata, but is just as likely to have led to their destruction. From the tenth century onwards, and increasingly in the nineteenth and twentieth centuries, Londoners have been digging away strata to construct cellars. Cellaring affects almost the whole of the interior of the walled city, removing a minimum of three metres of deposits. As one moves away from the centre of the city so more and more uncellared sites are found, but in general there is also a decrease in the depth of stratigraphy. Even where cellars have removed all horizontal Saxon levels, pits, cellars, wells and quarries can be expected to survive, even if they too have been truncated.

Useful records were made during the nineteenth century and earlier in the twentieth century by antiquarians and others who recorded traces of buildings of Roman or medieval date. No such records exist for Anglo-Saxon structures, nor could they be expected before the methods of excavating and recording ephemeral timber structures were developed, during the 1930s. To recognise an earth-dug rubbish pit or the post-holes or sleeper beam slots of a timber building is much more difficult than to record a stone wall or a stone-lined pit or well. This means that virtually no stratigraphic evidence for Saxon London was available until after the Second World War. At that time two teams started to record stratigraphy in advance of rebuilding. The best known is that of the Roman and Medieval London Excavation Committee (RMLEC), under its field director Professor Grimes, who was at that time Director of the London Institute of Archaeology. The work of this team came to national attention with the discovery of the Mithraeum on the east bank of the Walbrook. Saxon sites at St Bride's in Fleet Street, St Alban Wood Street,

Cannon Street, Addle Lane and just outside Cripplegate were excavated and the principal results summarised in a book, *The Archaeology of Roman and Medieval London*, published in 1968. Less well-known is the work of the Guildhall Museum who employed a lone field archaeologist. This post was filled first by Ivor Noel-Hume, who later went on to work in Colonial Williamsburg and became a founding father of American Historical Archaeology, and then by Peter Marsden, whose contribution to the study of Roman London is well-known through his popular books and a monograph on the Roman Forum (Marsden 1980; 1987). The conditions under which Noel-Hume and Marsden were working meant that only isolated blocks of stratigraphy could be examined, normally pits, wells and cellars. Nevertheless, over a thousand groups of finds from stratified contexts were collected and documented and a significant proportion of these date to the late Saxon period.

During the 1960s, as the pace of redevelopment and the public awareness of the archaeological destruction which it caused increased, larger excavations became possible, such as those on the site of the Huggin Hill Bathhouse (where all deposits later than the second century had been removed in antiquity), the Billingsgate Bathhouse (whose crucial evidence for the end of the Roman settlement is summarised by Marsden in his book, *Roman London*), and the Governor's Palace. Many of these sites should have produced evidence for late Saxon or medieval occupation, but the attitude of many archaeologists at that time towards post-Roman archaeology can be judged by the report on an excavation at Bush Lane House in Cannon Street, where Saxon and later features are shown in the final excavation report merely as intrusions destroying the Roman remains. To be fair, however, on a companion excavation just inside Aldgate the Saxon features were excavated, recorded and the associated artefacts impeccably published.

In 1973, the destruction of the late medieval Baynard's Castle and the discovery of the Roman Riverside Wall behind it created a climate favourable to rescue archaeology in London. National and local funds were used to set up a large field team in the Guildhall Museum. In 1974, with the amalgamation of the Guildhall and London Museums, this team became the Department of Urban Archaeology (DUA) of the new Museum of London. The DUA began an ambitious campaign of rescue archaeology in which excavations began on thirteen sites, some extensive. Many of these sites were on the medieval waterfront, in the middle of the Thames in the Saxon period, but Saxon strata were discovered on inland sites. The pace of excavation has continued ever since and at the time of writing is increasing. Analysis of the results of these excavations and their dissemination through publications quickly began to lag behind excavation and much of the information included in this book has been gathered in the course of producing a report on a backlog of unpublished DUA sites, excavated between 1974 and 1982. Means of publishing the results of current excavations quickly are still being sought but the public can consult the unpublished archive in the Museum of London Records Department.

Not all field archaeology took place inside the city walls. The Southwark and Lambeth Archaeological Excavation Committee excavated many sites in Southwark and made several important discoveries, not least a channel which may be that cut by order of King Cnut in 1016. North of the river archaeological results for the Saxon period were disappointing, apart from salvage excavations at The Treasury carried out under great difficulties in 1961. In April 1983 the professional units working in the London area were amalgamated to form the Department of Greater London Archaeology (DGLA) based in the Museum of London. Soon afterwards, starting in 1985, the luck of the north London archaeologists changed. Remarkable discoveries began to be made following the excavation at Jubilee Hall near Covent Garden.

Many of the initial results of these excavations will be mentioned here but the full impact of this work will only be felt once the post-excavation analysis which is now under way is completed. Not only is there a backlog but also new finds are being made every year. Each one helps to fill in more of the picture and some, such as the discovery of the amphitheatre in Guildhall Yard, cause a re-appraisal of what was previously believed about the topography of London. So long as re-development continues, and archaeologists are able to keep one step ahead of it, there will never be a definitive archaeology of Saxon London.

The study of Saxon London through field archaeology is still in its infancy but artefacts recognised as being of Anglo-Saxon date have been recorded for over a century. Unfortunately, many early finds apparently no longer exist and we have to work with either verbal descriptions or illustrations. These can be misleading. To give an example, a strange pot was recorded from the site of the Houses of Parliament in 1847. On the basis of the existing record, an engraving, it could well have been an Anglo-Saxon burial urn. However, by chance the actual vessel turned up a few years ago and passed onto John Clark of the Museum of London. He discovered that it was a peasant pot from the Indian sub-continent and probably not of any great age.

Another problem is that even when artefacts themselves survive, they were not recovered under the sort of controlled conditions to be found on an archaeological excavation. At least one hoard of Anglo-Saxon coins is recorded as coming from a site known to have been the residence of a nineteenth-century numismatist. Either the record of discovery became confused or perhaps the numismatist accidentally lost part of his collection. Whatever the explanation, without this extra knowledge those coins would have been accepted as archaeological evidence (even if of relatively poor quality).

It is unfortunate, but only to be expected, that some of the most interesting Saxon finds from London were found by chance before the importance of establishing their archaeological context could have been realised. These include several pieces of high-quality metalwork, such as a gold filigree and enamel brooch from Dowgate Hill and a silver and niello decorated sword pommel from Fetter Lane. There is no doubt, however, that these pieces were found on their respective sites. Two particular finds are much more dubious but, if genuine, are of even greater importance. These are complete jars of types made in what is now northern France or southern Belgium in the late sixth to early seventh centuries, which would indicate some sort of contact between the inhabitants of London and the kingdom of the Franks. The implications of these finds will be reiterated below, but it cannot be emphasised too strongly that they could turn out, like the Westminster pot mentioned above, to be relatively recent imports.

Evidence gleaned from unstratified artefacts is therefore always of lesser quality than that from excavations, but there is one advantage which these finds have. Chance finds are discovered wherever the ground is being disturbed, not just where archaeologists think an excavation might be productive. They are also potentially a source of information about areas whose present archaeological potential is low or non-existent, because earth-moving has been on such a scale that no stratigraphy remains, or where archaeological levels probably survive but are unlikely to be disturbed in the near future.

One problem with using chance finds is that the Anglo-Saxons had a much less distinctive material culture than either the Romano-Britons before them or their medieval descendants. They used pottery and implements made out of bone, tools of iron and decorative metalwork of copper alloy or precious metal. However, the number of finds from a typical excavation of an Anglo-Saxon settlement is far lower than that from either earlier or later ones. Furthermore, many of the artefacts they used are only known to be of Anglo-Saxon date because they were found in a stratified deposit of that date. The finds themselves are quite often not distinctive. In fact the most useful finds have proved to be pottery, clay loom weights, coins and decorated metalwork.

Potsherds are useful because they are relatively common and because they had little value, either to their original owners once the vessel they came from was broken or to collectors or museum curators. There is little advantage to a finder in lying about the findspot, which definitely takes place when finds with a monetary value are concerned. Another reason for using pottery is that there were great changes in the sources of pottery used throughout the Saxon period. Pots had a short useful life, unlike decorative metalwork which might be passed from generation to generation or recycled. Therefore, if a potsherd is found on a site it is most likely to have been discarded soon after breakage. Unless there is reason to believe that earth which might contain potsherds has been dumped on the site, the likelihood is that the site was occupied during the period in which that sort of pot was current. Single finds might have other explanations – potsherds could be spread on the fields with manure, for example – but the more finds there are the more likely they are to reveal the site of a Saxon settlement.

We can infer much about the appearance of the London area in the Saxon period through the use of a suite of techniques known as 'environmental archaeology'. In acidic soils, for example, pollen grains are preserved. The identity and analysis of these grains will reveal the amount of woodland and cultivated ground in the vicinity. A study of river silts will reveal the changing position of the tidal head of the Thames caused by the shift in the relative sea level since the end of the Roman period. Sieving of soil from Saxon rubbish pits or floor levels will reveal what plants and animals were used by the Anglo-Saxons as well as further details of the local environment. All of these techniques need deposits which are securely dated to the Saxon period and which are free from contamination from later material. For this reason, despite the enormous potential in this field (especially as many of the crucial questions about the period concern agriculture and the environment), there are as yet few results.

Coins are rare finds in the Anglo-Saxon period. From the end of the fourth century through to the beginning of the seventh century they were not used at all, or at least none are known to have been minted in England. From the early seventh century onwards, however, coins gradually came into use. The process by which England adopted a monetary economy is an interesting one and London seems to have played an important part in it. The study of coins enlightens us about Saxon London in several ways. First, a study of the coins which were minted in London, or which might conceivably have been minted there, shows the relative output of the London mint and others. It also reflects the political outlook of London. For example, who was claiming control over it at different times? Furthermore, the quality of the metal used for the coins reflects the state of the economy (although apparently not in a direct fashion). Coins are also useful in plotting the extent of settlement at different periods and, when they occur in hoards, can indicate periods of instability such as those brought about by Viking raids in the ninth to eleventh centuries. The total quantity of coins known from the London mint or found within the London area is a tiny fraction of what must originally have been minted or used and there will always be doubt about the reliability of this small sample when trying to say something about the way coins were used in the Saxon period.

The final type of evidence that I use here is that of place-names. Only a dozen or so places in Middlesex or Surrey have Anglo-Saxon names which were recorded before the eleventh century, and many of these are to be found in documents which have been copied and modified through the centuries so that we are not sure that the name found in a thirteenth-century copy of a tenth-century charter was in the original, and even less certain as to whether the name was 'modernised' by the scribe who copied the document. However, many hundred place-names to be found in the two counties, and several to be found in central London itself, have a form which suggests that they were originally given in the Anglo-Saxon period, or at the latest in the first few decades of Norman rule. How much can be said of conditions in the Saxon period by the use of place-names is debatable and the names, especially if only late spellings survive, are open to many interpretations. Perhaps the most telling of these changes is in the name 'Aldwych'. Originally this name denoted an area along the Strand where Drury Lane branched off to the north-west. It had fallen out of use by the beginning of this century but was resurrected to name the new crescent constructed at the southern end of Kingsway. It was thought most likely that the name originally meant old 'wich' — a name often given to a dairy farm (many *-wich* place-names can be found around the coast of Essex, for example) — but is now thought almost certainly to record the folk memory of the original Saxon town, *Lundenwic,* which we now know to have been centred on that area.

Part One

A history of Saxon London

Using all the available sources – documents, place-names and artefacts as well as the conventional results of excavation – a coherent image of London in the Saxon period can be assembled. In many areas this image is faint or may prove to be incorrect, but so long as there are archaeological deposits to be excavated and new ways of looking at old discoveries there is always the possibility of getting closer to the truth.

There are two ways of looking at the information. We can examine different aspects through time, such as the use of the countryside or changing fashions in clothing. But there are such major differences between London at the end of the Roman period and at the beginning of the Norman period that we first have to look at the evidence chronologically.

The Saxon period is conventionally divided by archaeologists into three parts. The early or pagan Saxon period starts at some point in the fourth or fifth century (opinion is divided over exactly when) and ends at some point in the seventh century following the adoption of Christianity. Here too the exact date is unclear since different areas adopted Christianity at different times. This mid-Saxon period ends in the ninth century and is defined archaeologically by the introduction of new types of pottery, many thrown on the wheel. The late Saxon period is equally difficult to define archaeologically. While logically it ought to end in 1066 with the defeat of the last Anglo-Saxon king, the Norman conquest is rarely discernible in archaeological evidence and artefacts cannot usually be dated more closely than *c.* 1050–1150.

These periods are simply a shorthand way to divide the Anglo-Saxon period into parts which can be more easily considered. The problem is that the events that archaeologists use to divide the period are not universally agreed, nor do those events occur at the same time in different areas. Ideally we would talk in terms of calendar years, but the evidence which can be used to provide an absolute date to excavated finds or sites is so incomplete that this is not yet possible. I will therefore use these terms freely in this book while warning the reader to beware of taking them too seriously. After all, Alfred the Great was born in mid-Saxon times and died in the late Saxon period. Historians have the same problem with Anglo-Saxon chronology but are generally baffled by the archaeological terminology, especially as it is used in slightly different ways by different people. Other terms which may crop up in this book or in the archaeological literature are 'migration period', which is used to describe sites or artefacts dating to the late fourth to seventh centuries and has the advantage of not suggesting the racial origins of the creators of the data; 'early medieval', a term whose use is totally confused in archaeology and whose meaning has to be decided by studying the context in which it was written; and 'Saxo-Norman', a term used mainly by pottery specialists to describe the date of material made between the last few decades of Anglo-Saxon rule and the middle of the twelfth century.

1 London in the late fourth century

Before we can consider the fate of London at the end of the Roman occupation it is necessary to review the state of our knowledge of the late Roman town (*see* Fig. 2). Documentary sources for this period are few, but we do know that in the early fourth century London had been renamed Augusta, a sign of Imperial favour, and briefly had its own mint. For the remaining years of the Roman occupation Britain had no mint and relied on imported coinage. The only surviving monument from this period is the city wall, which seems to have been started around the beginning of the third century. Parts of the defences are of fourth-century date, for example the circular bastions on the eastern side of the city, one of which can be seen by the White Tower in the Tower of London. Also within the Tower is a stretch of wall which formed part of the Roman riverside wall. Originally built around the middle of the third century, this stretch was rebuilt at the end of the fourth century. A study of the surviving fragment, built from fresh sandstone rather than the reused masonry characteristic of the bastions, certainly shows that there can have been no suspicion by its builders that the Empire would abandon not only London but the whole British province within a decade.

Despite the huge scale of the later Roman defences there is little corresponding evidence from within the walls. Excavation after excavation reveals the same sequence. The town was teeming with buildings and industry until some point in the later second or early third century, after which the whole pattern of streets and properties was changed. This is normally represented by the demolition of whatever buildings had been on the site and the dumping of a thick deposit of dark soil over the rubble (*see* Fig. 3). Not only private dwellings were affected but also public buildings, like the baths found at Huggin Hill, on the steep slope south of the relatively flat ground around St Paul's Cathedral.

No archaeologist today denies that London underwent a significant change during this period but there is considerable debate about what exactly this change was, its timing and speed and in particular about the size of the resident population. The main reason for this uncertainty is that the latest levels on most sites are the most disturbed by cellars, terracing, pit digging and other later activity. Only where deposits con-

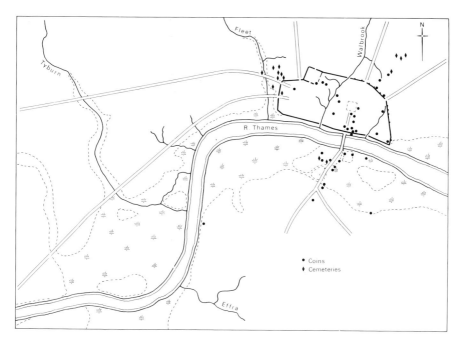

FIG. 2 Archaeological evidence for settlement in and around London in the late fourth century, *c.* 370 and later.

FIG. 3 A typical 'dark earth' deposit, from Milk Street, London. Note that where not destroyed by later pits the mosaic pavement is well-preserved. (Museum of London)

tinued to accumulate, such as the sides of the Walbrook valley and the strip of land immediately behind the riverside wall, is there archaeological evidence in any quantity. Elsewhere our knowledge of what happened in later Roman London is based on a study of artefacts which have been preserved by being reburied in later pits and which can be assumed to have originally been discarded on floors or in pits which no longer survive. The most eloquent testimony comes from the coins. Later Roman coins were of small value and were therefore used in large numbers and were of little consequence if lost. They are therefore found in profusion in the remains of later Roman settlements and London is no exception. Even where all later Roman occupation levels have been destroyed there is usually a scatter of later third and early to mid-fourth-century coins in later deposits. However, the number of later fourth-century coins is much lower than would be predicted on the basis of these late third to mid fourth-century finds. The coinage suggests that London went into a decline at this time, relative to many other Roman settlements. The successful settlements of the later fourth century were the large, sprawling villages, numerous peasant farmsteads, a few of the once ubiquitous villa estates and the forts of the Saxon Shore, places such as Portchester in Hampshire or Bradwell-on-Sea in Essex.

During the second century the army became less in evidence in lowland Britain. Fortresses in the south and east were abandoned and their garrisons redeployed elsewhere, for example in Wales and Scotland. This appears to have been the case in London, where two sides of an old fort at Cripplegate were included into the city wall circuit (Grimes 1968, 15–39). However, sea-borne raiders from outside the Empire started to become a serious problem during the third century and in order to counter their attacks a series of forts and associated structures was constructed and manned during the later third and fourth centuries. In the late fourth century they were under the control of the Count of the Saxon Shore. The nearest fort to London was at Bradwell, at the tip of the Dengie peninsula in Essex, but a fortified watch tower or 'signal station' excavated at Shadwell, just to the east of the city, may have been part of this reorganised defensive system and seems to have been constructed in the middle of the third century.

When the army was withdrawn by Honorius in 410 the defence of the province would have been left in the hands of the *civitates*, the civil administration based on the *civitas* capitals, of which London was one. A story preserved by both the British and the English is that the early fifth-century rulers of Britannia hired barbarian soldiers to replace the army but that they rebelled, took over the administration and opened up the province to their kinsmen from Saxony, Jutland and the region then known as Angeln, at the mouth of the Elbe. Three hundred years later the English thought of themselves as belonging to three races: Angles, Saxons and Jutes. Archaeological evidence too suggests that many aspects of the early English material culture originated in that area of north-west Europe, although attempts to use artefacts such as brooches, or customs such as burial rites, to show the racial makeup of particular communities show instead that early English culture was hybrid. It certainly had Germanic prototypes, but was developed in England.

London may or may not have had a large population in the late fourth century, but it was undoubtedly occupied and continued to have an official function, as shown by the riverside wall in the Tower of London. Its fate in the early fifth century is even less clear. Even in those areas where occupation evidence survives, for example at the foot of the hill between London Bridge and the Tower, excavations have failed to find positive evidence for occupation after *c*. 400. This is not helped by the fact that the province stopped using coinage in *c*. 400 and that it is most likely that mass-produced pottery ceased to be made around the same time. Practically the only way to demonstrate that a Romano-British settlement was occupied in the fifth century is to excavate a sequence of buildings and show that the earlier part of this sequence dates to the late fourth century. Then, the date of the succeeding structures can be estimated. This has been done at the towns of Wroxeter and Verulamium (the predecessor of St Albans) and at the villas of Rivenhall in Essex and Latimer in the Chilterns. In London, on the other hand, there is positive evidence that some areas went out of use. Immediately north of the old fish market at Billingsgate a building with a bath block was excavated in 1968 (Marsden 1980). It was first built in the late second or early third century and continued in use to the end of the fourth century. Refuse on the floors must have accumulated after the buildings had been abandoned, or were being used for less prestigious purposes. Coins found with the refuse date to the very end of the fourth century, but rather than later buildings overlying these deposits there was instead a layer of tiles, which had fallen when the rafters rotted and had not been touched since. If occupation had continued in the area it is almost certain that the more complete tiles would have been taken away to be reused as walling, flooring or on another roof. Within this tile layer was found a badly corroded brooch of Germanic type. Indeed, the closest parallel comes from a burial in an Anglo-Saxon cemetery at Mitcham in Surrey. Current thinking suggests that the brooch was made in the middle of the fifth century, although the Mitcham example accompanied a burial of the late fifth century. Thus a site just inside one of the main entrances to London, the bridge linking London to Southwark, saw no activity at all between *c*. 400 and perhaps the end of the fifth century.

The *Anglo-Saxon Chronicle* has an entry under the year 457 which states that the British fought against the English at a place called *Crecganford* (which is thought by place-name specialists to be Crayford,

in Kent) and then retreated to London. On the basis of the Billingsgate
bathhouse site, and the lack of any contradictory evidence from elsewhere
in the city, it seems that the city was already an empty shell, useful in
times of threat but no longer a living settlement.

At present we can only speculate about the change in political fortunes
which seems to have lead to the abandonment of London while Verulamium
was still flourishing. When St Germanus of Auxerre visited Britain in
428/9 to combat the Pelagian heresy, the one place which we know he
visited was the shrine to St Alban, probably located close to the present
St Alban's Abbey.

The difficulty in identifying settlement sites or burials of the sub-
Roman Britons contrasts sharply with the archaeological profile of the
early Anglo-Saxon settlers. These people were predominantly farmers and
most of our evidence comes from the remains of their farmsteads or the
cemeteries which were attached to them. However, one of the characteristic
features of a fifth to seventh-century Anglo-Saxon cemetery is the presence
of burials accompanied by weapons, ranging from the large single-sided
knife, or *Seax*, to the spear and ultimately the shield and sword. This
apparent emphasis on warfare is also reflected in their literature and
historial records and has dominated discussion of the Anglo-Saxon settlement of England and the relationship of the Germanic settlers to the
indigenous population.

It is perhaps odd that despite the political turmoil of the fifth and sixth
centuries, and the undoubted importance of fighting in Anglo-Saxon
society, the Anglo-Saxons do not seem to have developed any system of
defensive enclosures, which are one of the most distinctive features of
Celtic Britain before the Roman conquest. Many hill forts were forcibly
abandoned during the Roman occupation but were reoccupied, albeit
mostly on a smaller scale than before, during the later fourth, fifth and
sixth centuries. The only earthwork in the London area to which a fifth-
or sixth-century date has been ascribed is the bank and ditch known as
Grim's Dyke at Pear Tree Wood, Stanmore. However, the actual date of
this earthwork is unknown, except that it is of Roman or later date,
perpetuates a line begun in the Iron Age in Pinner and runs just inside the
boundary between Hertfordshire and Middlesex, which did not achieve
its Saxon administrative significance until the tenth century. Anglo-Saxon
military strategy did not therefore incorporate garrisons, siege or any of
the other notions by which a defensive enclosure like London's wall might
be of use.

Two other features of the Roman city might have attracted attention in
the succeeding era. First, the timber bridge linking London to Southwark,
which has recently been demonstrated to have been originally constructed
in the late first century, would have been a convenient crossing point so
long as it continued to survive in good repair. However, although it is

assumed that the bridge was incorporated into the defences in the mid-third century there is no archaeological evidence to confirm this. Some sort of Roman occupation continued on the gravel eyots which formed Southwark until at least the late fourth century, but the settlement, like that in the city, cannot be demonstrated to have continued into the fifth century. Apart from a single mid-sixth-century coin of Justinian found on the site of a medieval and later inn at King Harry Yard in the nineteenth century, there is no evidence for any human activity at Southwark until the late ninth or early tenth century, when a coin of Alfred the Great was lost at St Thomas Street.

The second Roman feature which may have attracted attention later was the harbour. Excavations along the city waterfront have shown that the timber quays which were characteristic of the first to third centuries were not replaced once the city wall was constructed in the mid-third century. Examination of a large quantity of artefacts recovered from the old river channel in front of the quays at Billingsgate confirm that rubbish deposition in the river tailed off at the same time as the latest evidence for use of the quays. The problem of the location of late Roman London's harbour facilities has not yet been solved. One possibility is that the reduced volume of traffic could be catered for by small wharves in front of watergates, of which Billingsgate may have been one. There is no evidence so far to show that any of these gates (whose names are well documented in the twelfth century and later) was a feature of the Roman town. Alternatively, there may have been a port further up or down the Thames.

Whatever the attraction of the late Roman harbour facilities along the city waterfront, if any, the disadvantage of having to carry goods inside the walls would also have had to be considered. Facilities would have to have been concentrated around the watergates. There is no archaeological evidence for fifth to sixth-century ports in Britain and every reason to suppose that the reduced overseas traffic of the period could be catered for by natural harbours, such as those which abounded around the coasts of Essex and Kent. It is also important to bear in mind that the coastline of south-east England has changed considerably from the Roman period to the present day, some channels silting up and others opening. This is not to say that the port of London was not an important aspect of the rebirth of the town, only that we are not in a position to evaluate it.

The seventh century is taken by archaeologists to form the divide between early Saxon and mid-Saxon times. The crucial difference was that at the beginning of the century people still buried their dead in the same manner as they had done since the fifth century and lived in the same type of settlements. By the end of the century there had been a radical change of land use, resulting in the abandonment of many areas of early settlement. There had also been a major change in religious beliefs, whose main manifestation in the archaeological record was the eventual disappearance of burials accompanied by grave goods and their replacement by inhumation cemeteries where the majority of burials had no grave goods, except for items of clothing. These graves were laid out regularly and orientated east-west. The cause of the latter change, if not ultimately the former as well, was the conversion of the Anglo-Saxons to Christianity. London played an important role in the conversion and it is said that Pope Gregory's original plan was to create a new ecclesiastical province for the English with its centre at London. Events in the early seventh century did not allow this plan to be carried out and by the time it was logistically possible the position of Canterbury at the head of the English Church had been assured by its tradition and sanctity. London had to make do with a bishopric, founded in 604, seven years after St Augustine and his mission arrived in Kent.

These events have stimulated historians to ponder on the significance of the intended choice of London. The organisation of the fifth to seventh-century Roman Church was modelled on that of the late Empire, so that long after imperial control had ceased in Gaul, for example, the bishops continued to operate from the *civitas* capitals and to have dioceses which mirrored those of the old civil administration. When England was brought back within the Roman Christian fold there may have been an attempt to recreate the late Roman civil administrative hierarchy. Alternatively, since there was a strong tradition in the Roman Church that a bishop should be based in a town, it may be that Canterbury, Rochester, London and the other centres chosen as the seats of seventh-century bishops, were once again urban settlements, or at least the closest substitute that could be found in England at the time.

No trace has been found of the early Saxon cathedral of St Paul. By analogy with other English cathedrals, in particular those at Winchester and Canterbury, it is assumed that the Saxon church lay close to, but not immediately underneath, its medieval successor. The position in London is further confused by the fact that the medieval church was swept away completely following the Great Fire of 1666. For various reasons it is more likely that the Saxon cathedral lay to the south rather than to the north of Wren's cathedral, which is more or less on top of the medieval structure. Foundations excavated in the nineteenth century at Rochester, and interpreted as those of the seventh-century cathedral church, lie immediately underneath the western doorway of the Norman church. Even if anything survives of the seventh-century cathedral at London it is unlikely to be available for archaeological excavation in the near future. Excavations in the surrounding area, for example at Knightrider Street (Nos. 29−31, The Horn Tavern) and St Paul's churchyard (Nos. 1−5) suggest that the whole of this area has been subject to severe terracing, removing all archaeological levels down to the natural gravel. However,

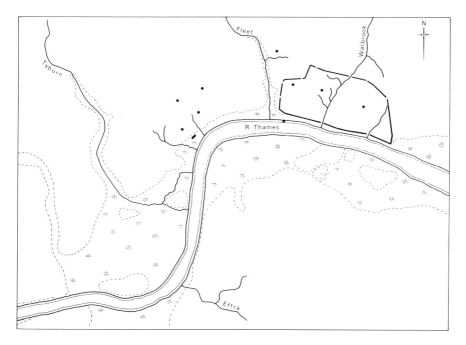

FIG. 4 Archaeological evidence for occupation in London in the early mid-Saxon period. The black rectangle marks the position of the late seventh century waterfront discovered in 1988 at York Buildings.

the fills of some of the medieval and later pits of Knightrider Street produced sherds of early or mid-Saxon pottery, a hint that conventual buildings may have once existed to the south of the cathedral.

A few other excavations in the city have produced sherds of similar pottery. Some from Peter's Hill were found in spreads of rubble brought onto the site to form the foundations of an eleventh or twelfth-century street. This site is immediately south of that at Knightrider Street while a third site, where the riverside wall crossed the old course of Thames Street, produced sherds of mid-Saxon pottery in a context which suggests that this part of the city was at that time a freshwater marsh. A few finds of metalwork from the city are probably of early to mid-Saxon date, for example a broken spearhead from Poultry (the eastern end of Cheapside), but the only other finds of pottery are a single sherd found in a deposit dumped on the foreshore at New Fresh Wharf in the eleventh century and three complete pots in the collections of the Museum of London (*see* Fig. 5). All three are unusual (in that they were made in northern France or southern Belgium) and therefore suspect. Complete pots have been collectors' items for centuries and many collectors were careless about recording the provenance of their finds. It is quite possible that these three pots are genuine finds, but until similar finds are made under controlled circumstances they must remain under suspicion.

The majority of excavations in the city produce no evidence concerning the city in the early to mid-Saxon periods and the lack of earlier finds in later pit-fills and the lack of pits or wells do strongly imply that most of the city was uninhabited. This lack of evidence means that we do not know what the city was used for if it was not occupied. Nowhere, for example, has a soil horizon datable to the period been recognised, while the evidence for the condition of Roman masonry structures is equivocal. Most Roman stone walls were robbed in the late Saxon period but this need not mean that their walls stood above ground. They may well have been encountered during pit digging and then robbed piecemeal.

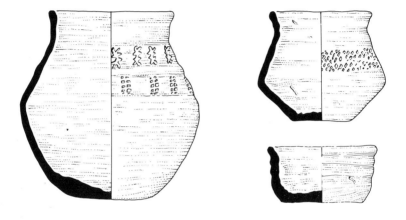

FIG. 5   Three imported pots found in the walled city of London, probably made in northern France in the late sixth or early seventh century. (Drawn by Anne Jenner)

Roman London therefore survived to the very end of the fourth century but at that time buildings were abandoned. The latest activity took place in the south-east corner of the city, under what is now the Tower of London. This, together with a hoard of late fourth or early fifth century gold coins and a silver ingot from the same area, suggests that the treasury may have been located in this part of the city. Nowhere, however, is there any positive evidence for occupation extending into the fifth century, let alone any later.

2 The Strand settlement

There is no historical evidence for the existence of a settlement at London in the sixth century but Bede, writing in Northumbria in the 730s, referred back to the early years of the seventh century when London was chosen as the seat of the bishop of the East Saxons. He described London as a 'mart of many nations'. This description could refer to the London of Bede's day or to the situation in 604. However, a charter of the 670s mentions the port of London and we can be fairly certain that Bede's description applied at least to the later seventh-century town.

Evidence for Saxon occupation within the city walls is slight until the late ninth century or later. Despite the poor survival of the archaeological levels of this date, the absence of pits and wells in the walled city suggests that any early or mid-Saxon settlement was very small. Nevertheless, until 1984 it was the consensus of archaeological opinion that the secular community, which historical records tell us existed alongside the ecclesiastical one, must have been small enough to fit in between the cathedral and the river, the only area in which any archaeological traces had been found. Now, however, it is believed that the main settlement of mid-Saxon London lay outside the walled city and was of a considerable size.

Southwark has no evidence of settlement of this date, despite a large campaign of excavation (*see* page xi). Much of Lambeth would have been uninhabitable marshland and seems to have remained so into the sixteenth century, while excavations on the site of the medieval abbey at Bermondsey, at the edge of the marshland, suggest that it was agricultural land during the mid-Saxon period, although a settlement must lie nearby. North of the river there has been little opportunity for excavation to the east of the city and what work has been possible has shown that extensive areas have had their archaeological levels destroyed by late medieval gravel quarrying. Where levels survive they show that there was no occupation after the use of the area as a cemetery in the late Roman period until the late eleventh or twelfth century. No sites along the line of the Roman or Saxon riverside have been excavated but it is suspected, considering the underlying geology, that the area would have consisted of mudflats until it was reclaimed and the drainage controlled by a continuous river wall in the medieval period. To the north of the city a similar pattern of land use has been found at Spitalfields, while sites at Clerkenwell, Cloth Fair (opposite St Bartholomew's Priory) and St Bartholomew's

Hospital confirm the documentary evidence that these sites were agricultural until acquired by religious institutions in the twelfth century. Most have produced some evidence for prehistoric or Roman activity, confirming that if early to mid-Saxon settlements had been present then some trace should have survived.

At the northern end of Tottenham Court Road an excavation on the site of Tottenhall, a medieval manor, produced a small group of early Saxon potsherds from a medieval ploughsoil. Somewhere close by must have been a settlement, probably dating to the sixth century, but no actual settlement traces were found. This is the closest known early Saxon settlement to the city but it would not be surprising to find similar scattered agricultural settlements throughout the London area.

Further south, traces of mid-Saxon settlement are plentiful, although until recently only one site, the Treasury in Whitehall, had been examined by archaeological excavation. This site, first thought to be that of a large timber hall, the residence of a local *thegn* surrounded by fields, is now thought to be on the edge of a large trading settlement extending along the riverside to the Fleet. If you stand in Whitehall, looking north towards Trafalgar Square, it requires a huge leap of imagination to remember that in the eighth century the riverbank would have run immediately under your feet. A Roman road ran in front of you, underneath the Strand and Piccadilly. To either side in the early Roman period may have been isolated burials and a scatter of Roman artefacts suggests that these burials were interspersed with farms. To the north-east is St Martin-in-the-Fields church, first recorded in the thirteenth century.

In the late thirteenth century the rumour of treasure trove began a riot which lead to the desecration of consecrated ground (*see* page 61). Five hundred years later, while rebuilding the front of the church, a stone coffin was found, presumably a reused Roman sarcophagus. Inside were two glass bowls (*see* Fig. 6) and some 'ashes'. Whether this term should imply that the coffin contained a cremation rather than decayed bone is unknown, but the bowls were acquired by Sir Hans Sloane, whose collection formed the nucleus of the British Museum, and are today to be found in the Department of Medieval and Later Antiquities. They are of a type well-known from Anglo-Saxon burials and are thought to be of late sixth or early seventh-century date. This find lends some credence to the thirteenth-century chronicle and suggests that there may have been other, richer burials close by. A gold ring, also in the British Museum, was found nearby in Garrick Street (*see* Fig. 7). Its decoration appears to incorporate a cross and this, together with the filigree technique, suggests that it is seventh-century or later. Whether it too came from a burial is impossible to tell. Further finds, but of a domestic nature, have been made to the north, underneath the National Gallery, in excavations in advance of the National Gallery extension and close to Leicester Square underground station.

FIG. 6 One of two glass bowls from the St Martin-in-the-Fields burial. (British Museum)

FIG. 7 The Garrick Street ring, dated to the mid or late Saxon period. (Illustration after VCH. Photo: British Museum)

Turning east along the Strand one can see that the road runs along the crest of a hill. To the left (north) the land slopes gently upwards but on the right (south) there is a steep drop followed by an almost level terrace. The latter terrace is all made ground, of late medieval and later date, and the steep slope originally formed a cliff leading down to the river. On the site of the Savoy palace stands a sixteenth-century chapel which illustrates the original lie of the land. Nearby in 1924 were found some loom weights, a complete pot dated to the seventh century and a sherd of a decorated jar of Ipswich-type ware, a type probably of later seventh, eighth or early ninth-century date. These finds were discussed by Sir Mortimer Wheeler in 1935. He interpreted them as being evidence for a Saxon farm. Isolated finds have been made on either side of the road but the most worthy of note was made on the site of Jubilee Hall in 1985. This was the first of the recent batch of sites to be excavated and revealed a single burial, which was clearly earlier that at least two phases of domestic occupation (represented by pits, wells and the remains of ground-level timber buildings).

Further east one comes to the crescent known as Aldwych with Southampton Row and Kingsway running north from it. The name Aldwych was borrowed from the locality a little further east where a triangle of land used to be bounded by the Strand to the south and Drury Lane to the north. Traces of settlement have been found to the east of the Aldwych, the most easterly of which was a hoard of coins, hidden in the 840s, probably at the time of the Viking raid of 841. This hoard was buried at Hare Court, part of the Middle Temple in Fleet Street. Excavations at St Bride's Church, which lies further east on a small promontory overlooking the Thames, leave open the possibility that there may have been a church on the site at this period, although the earliest stone foundations discovered were probably of eleventh-century date. To the south, the whole area once formed the extensive mouth of the River Fleet and much was only reclaimed in the late medieval period. Excavation has shown that there would have been mudflats, crossed by channels. One medieval timber pile is thought to have been a reused boat timber and has been shown by dendrochronology to be of tenth-century date. Nevertheless, it seems that the mid-Saxon settlement avoided the area in favour of the harder ground to the west. Further evidence in favour of this view comes from recent excavations at the City of London Boys School, on the edge of the Fleet mouth in the mid-Saxon period. Roman pottery was found there, presumably washed in from occupation sites just below St Bride's, but the first post-Roman activity can be dated to the twelfth century. Similar 'negative' evidence comes from a site at Barnard's Inn, at the east end of High Holborn.

St Bride's Church would have been within sight of the walled city, but separated from it by the Fleet valley. Bridges or fords undoubtedly crossed this tributary, both below where Holborn Viaduct now runs and at Ludgate Circus. The state of these crossings by the seventh century is impossible to tell but no great engineering feat would have been needed to repair or rebuild them. Heading north, up Farringdon Street, one reaches the original crossing point of the Roman road which left London at Newgate and runs to the west, first as High Holborn, then as Oxford Street. Almost immediately one rejoins the street heading back west and finds St Andrew's Holborn. This church was described as the old wooden church of St Andrew in a charter of the mid-tenth century, parts of whose bounds we have just followed. Just how much of the area bordered by these two Roman roads and the Fleet was occupied in the mid-Saxon period is impossible to tell yet, but a remarkable proportion of the area should have archaeological levels surviving below the ground. Destruction has been greatest on properties fronting onto the main streets and so far no site actually fronting onto the Strand or Fleet Street has proved to have any archaeology left intact.

Much has been discovered in the last few years about the nature of this settlement. We now know that the majority of the buildings were rectangular, timber structures and that metalled areas which may have been yards existed alongside them. Their rubbish was either shovelled into old cesspits and wells or left as middens. Much remains to be discovered. We do not know, for example, whether there was a regular street grid or whether the buildings sat within separate properties. At the closely comparable settlement of Dorestad, on the Rhine delta, the settlement appears to have been divided into zones of differing land use: a mercantile zone next to the river lay in front of an agricultural one

To date, the earliest finds from this area, known for convenience as the Strand or Aldwych settlement, are possibly of sixth-century date and are concentrated in the centre of the later settlement, around Trafalgar Square. Seventh-century finds are more numerous but have the same distribution. However, by the ninth century the whole of the settlement seems to have been occupied (*see* Fig. 8). Some early Anglo-Saxon rural settlements also covered a considerable area. Where they have been closely studied it seems that they were composed of nuclei which were cyclically occupied, so that the total area inhabited at one time was smaller than the extent of the settlement evidence. The contrast between this settlement (and similar ones elsewhere in England) and the earlier rural settlements is therefore even greater than it might otherwise seem.

The latest material from the Strand settlement dates to the early ninth century, although another hoard, deposited in *c.* 870, was recovered from the bed of the Thames at the south end of Waterloo Bridge. The fate of the Strand settlement is therefore still surrounded by mystery. The historical events of the ninth century were fast-moving and themselves only poorly understood. First, there was apparently a decline in overseas trade, which

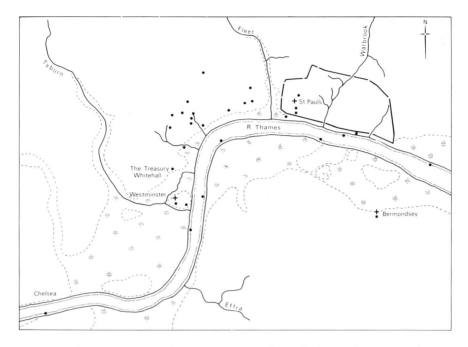

FIG. 8   Archaeological evidence for occupation in London in the later mid-Saxon period.

affected many of the large trading settlements of the North Sea coast. Settlements at Dorestad, Quentovic on the Quanche in northern France, Southampton and York as well as London all suffered the same fate, at more or less the same time (*see* Fig. 9). However, as far as is known there was no such drastic decline at Ipswich, where the mid-Saxon settlement underlies the later Saxon and medieval town, both of which seem to have been of similar size to the mid-Saxon town.

Second, from the late eighth century onwards England was once again subject to attack from seaborne raiders, this time from Scandinavia. Certainly, not all the Viking raids on England were recorded in historical records and there is no means of telling whether the recorded raids on London, in 841, 851 and 871, were the only ones or just the most memorable. Nevertheless, by the late 860s the Vikings had stepped up their assault on England (and the Continent) and in 870 killed King Edmund of East Anglia and later took over his kingdom. Four years later Burgred, king of Mercia, was ousted and replaced by a Viking nominee, Ceolwulf II. Half the kingdom of Mercia was taken by the Vikings, who used it as a base for raids into Wessex. London must have been affected by these changes taking place around it, but how?

In the ninth century trading settlements in the Viking sphere seem to have fared much better than those further south. Perhaps the best known example is that at Haithabu (Hedeby), the predecessor of Schleswig, on the Baltic coast. Not only is there no evidence for a sharp decline in size or number of settlements at this time, there is also some evidence for the growth of towns, such as Birka, in southern Sweden. If London had been absorbed into the Viking world then, like Ipswich, it may have flourished. However, in the 880s the tide turned against the Vikings and the English steadily regained territory, including London. The year 886 seems to have marked an important stage in this English recovery and during that year 'King Alfred occupied London; and all the English people that were not under subjections to the Danes submitted to him. And he then entrusted the borough to the control of Ealdorman Ethelred' (Whitelock 1968 No. 1, 183). A grant of 888/9 makes it clear that the main settlement at London was by then within the walls of the Roman city.

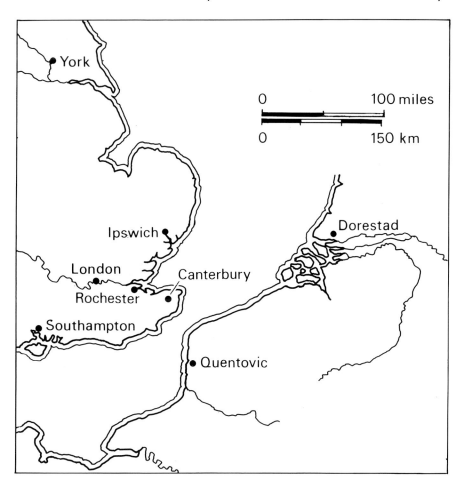

FIG. 9 Some of the international ports in the North Sea and English Channel in the ninth century. More sites almost certainly await discovery or, like Dunwich on the East Anglian coast, have completely disappeared. Canterbury was served by its outpost of Fordwich.

It is reasonably clear that until the middle of the ninth century the main secular settlement of London, *Lundenwic* in contemporary records, lay along the Strand and documentary evidence makes it equally clear that by *c*. 890 the focus had shifted to the walled city. The exact timing of the move, its precise causes and under whose control it took place are all unanswered questions.

In 857 a 'profitable little estate' in the 'town of London' situated by the west gates was acquired by the bishop of Worcester. The location of this estate is of considerable interest and most commentators have assumed, since there is no evidence that the Strand settlement was ever walled, that the gates referred to in this grant must therefore be those of the Roman city. At first one naturally thinks of Ludgate and Newgate as being the gates referred to, but it was said at the end of the sixteenth century that Newgate was constructed in the twelfth century. We now know the gate is Roman in origin and if it was 'new' in the twelfth century this must be because it had been rebuilt or unblocked at that time. It is just possible that Cripplegate or Aldersgate could be thought of as being west gates and if so this would have the effect of placing the estate inside the area of the Cripplegate fort. The previous holder of the estate was Ceolmund who gave his name to it, *Ceolmundinghaga*. The only ninth-century Ceolmund known was an ealdorman of Kent and there has long been a tradition that a royal palace lay in this part of the city, utilising remnants of the early Roman fort. The name Aldermanbury, 'enclosure of the ealdorman', suvives today and presumably must date back to at least the late tenth century, since the position of ealdorman was largely replaced by that of the earl in the early eleventh century. A further possibility is that Ceolmund's haga lay in the south-west corner of the city and that the west gates may have been in the demolished riverside wall. Wherever the estate was located, it was said to be profitable and therefore probably connected with trade rather than just an aristocratic residence. If it lay within the walls it therefore tentatively places the movement from the Strand to the city before the Viking takeover of Mercia. The Latin name used for London in this charter is probably a translation of *Lundenwic*, however, and this suggests either that the estate was in the Strand settlement or that the term *Lundenwic* was used to denote the trading settlement of London wherever it lay. Perhaps the most likely explanation would be that the estate lay at the eastern end of the Strand settlement, and for that reason was said to be by the west gates.

Further evidence comes from two documents, the first of which is a charter granting an estate called *Hwaetmundes stan* in London to Bishop Waerferth of Worcester in 888/9. The estate's boundaries are indicated by its dimensions, a street to the north and the city wall to the south. The grant allowed the bishop's men to trade within the estate but sought to regulate trade outside, on the public street or the *ripa emptoralis*, the riverside market. The later document is not a charter but a record of decisions taken by King Alfred at a council in Chelsea in 898/9. Two estates were granted, one to Waerferth and the other to Archbishop Plegmund, and in contrast to the earlier grant both recipients were also to have the right to moor ships along the width of their properties. In 1978 Tony Dyson, the historian attached to the DUA, published a paper in which he suggested, very plausibly, that the estate granted to Worcester in each case was the same (Dyson 1978). This enabled the descriptive information to be combined, leading to the identification of both estates on the ground (*see* Fig. 10). The later document revealed that the estates were close to *Aetheredes hid*, known from the twelfth century onwards as Queenhithe. The Ethelred after whom Queenhithe was originally named

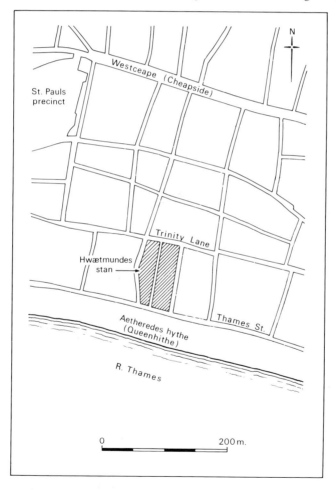

FIG. 10   The location of *Hwaetmundes stan* and the western street grid. Thames Street runs along the approximate position of the Roman riverside wall, which was still standing in the late ninth century.

must be the same man to whom Alfred entrusted London in 886, his son-in-law and joint grantor in the 888/9 grant, in which he styled himself *subregulus et patricus Merciorum*. It is likely that the extra rights granted in 898/9 were intended to give London's economy an extra boost, especially considering that the subject of the Chelsea council was the renewal of London.

Not only do the Queenhithe charters reveal royal interest in trade in London but they also hint that in the interval between the two documents new streets had been created. In the 888/9 charter only one street is mentioned, identifiable as a major east-west street known in the medieval period as Great Trinity Lane, Cloak Lane, Great St Thomas Lane and Knightrider Street. In the later document minor roads are mentioned which ran north to meet the public street. Two of these, Bread Street and Garlick Hill, have the distinction of being the southern ends of the only roads to lead all the way from the river to Cheapside. Such streets are likely to have been laid out before the area they crossed was densely occupied. This documentary evidence, together with a change in the name used for London from *Lundenwic* to *Lundenburh*, suggest that the walled city was by the late ninth century the centre not only for defence but for commerce too.

The archaeological evidence to compare with the historical data is inconclusive. Only one small area of the foreshore in the south-western part of the city has been excavated, at Baynard's Castle in 1974/5. This was some way away from Queenhithe and produced no evidence for activity earlier than the late eleventh to mid-twelfth century. The site of the *Hwaetmundes stan* estate has been excavated (it was the site of the Huggin Hill baths) but all levels later than the second century have been terraced away, including pits and other features which might have contained residual Saxon finds. The only direct archaeological observation of any relevance is that at Well Court, fronting onto Bow Lane. Here, a small fragment of the early street was excavated, together with fragments of timber buildings built at ground level and fronting onto the street (*see* Fig. 11).

The excavation established that Bow Lane was not on the line of a Roman street but lay on top of late Roman dark earth. Its position in relation to the later medieval and modern streets suggests that originally it had been quite wide but that encroachment from either side had considerably narrowed it. The first surface contained a large amount of reused Roman debris – fragments of tile and building stone – while later surfaces were made from gravel brought into the city or perhaps dug from deep pits cutting right through the earlier occupation levels. Unfortunately there were few other artefacts in the road metalling or in the silt above and all those found were likely to have been of Roman date. The earliest timber buildings were likewise without contemporary finds but were replaced by a building containing a bread oven (*see* Fig. 12) and sherds of

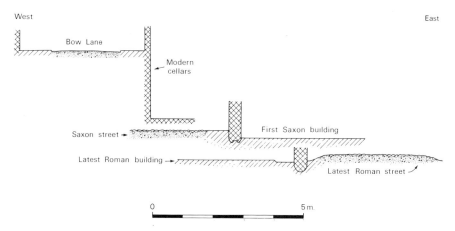

West   East

Bow Lane

Modern cellars

Saxon street →   First Saxon building

Latest Roman building →   Latest Roman street

0   5 m.

FIG. 11   The relationship of Bow Lane in the Saxon period to earlier and later streets. Whereas Saxon Bow Lane was laid over Roman buildings and ignored the Roman street, the modern Bow Lane is a direct successor of the Saxon street. It has either become narrower since the ninth century or has shifted slightly to the west.

FIG. 12   The foundations of a bread oven dating to the tenth or early eleventh century, Well Court. (Museum of London)

late Saxon pottery. The absence of Saxon finds from the first road metalling does not mean that the road is likely to be of Roman date, and is hardly surprising considering the size of the excavation, but it may imply that the street was laid out before any Saxon occupation in the area.

The only other relevant archaeological evidence comes from the discovery of pits, buildings and loose finds of ninth century date. The first piece of evidence is negative. There are very few finds of pottery or other artefacts from the city which have close parallels amongst the rapidly growing collection from the Strand settlement. Hundreds of late Saxon and medieval pits and wells have been recorded in the city but only one contains a find of mid-Saxon character, a single-handled comb from a pit at Lombard Street. This suggests that there was no wholesale movement of inhabitants of the Strand settlement into the city. However, since we do not know

FIG. 13   The range of pottery types produced in Late Saxon Shelly ware. (Museum of London)

precisely when the Strand settlement was abandoned this does not provide a fixed point for the chronology of the walled settlement. The earliest Saxon occupation recognised in the city is characterised by a type of pottery — Late Saxon Shelly ware, or LSS ware for short — which was still in use in the first half of the eleventh century (*see* Fig. 13). While this does not mean that it could not have been introduced in the mid-ninth century it does mean that there is no means of distinguishing a pit used at this time from one filled a century and a half later. The only way in which this problem will eventually be solved will be if it is possible to show either that LSS was used in the mid-ninth century, in which case there genuinely is no means of closely dating later Saxon occupation in the city, or by finding independently dated levels which show that it was not used, in which case ninth-century occupation in the city must have been sparse.

Loose finds of metalwork dated art-historically to the ninth century have been found in the city, although their suggested dates tend to fluctuate as opinion changes. They are sparse and in no case come from deposits which might have a ninth-century date. The only other relevant find is a hoard of coins found on a site at the eastern end of Cheapside, Bucklersbury, in the nineteenth century. This hoard, which no longer exists, was apparently composed solely of late coins of Alfred. If correctly recorded, such a hoard would probably have been deposited before the end of the ninth century.

Our knowledge of mid-Saxon London has changed so rapidly over such a short period of time that it is difficult to summarise the evidence. It is nevertheless certain that the London of Bede lay outside the walls of the Roman city and occupied an extensive tract of land. It existed in the seventh century, flourished during the eighth and early ninth centuries but ceased to exist before the end of the ninth century. It is also quite clear that large-scale occupation within the walled city started only after the Strand settlement had ceased to exist. Within this framework there is plenty of room for differences of opinion as to the actual dates of these events and their nature. Only further archaeological work can hope to narrow down the range of possibilities.

3 Late Saxon London

The documentary sources are surprisingly uninformative about tenth-century London (*see* Fig. 14). In his stimulating study of early medieval London, Professor Brooke of the University of Cambridge was able to trace many of the institutions of the medieval town back before the Norman conquest and, he argued, back before the Viking conquest in the early eleventh century. The tenth century was identified as a formative period, a conclusion with which subsequent archaeological work agrees. And yet there are fewer references to London in this century than in the previous one. This must partly be a case of no news being good news. The two occasions on which the city was mentioned in the *Anglo-Saxon Chronicle* were in 962, when a destructive fire burnt down St Paul's (it was rebuilt the same year) and in 982, when there was a great fire in

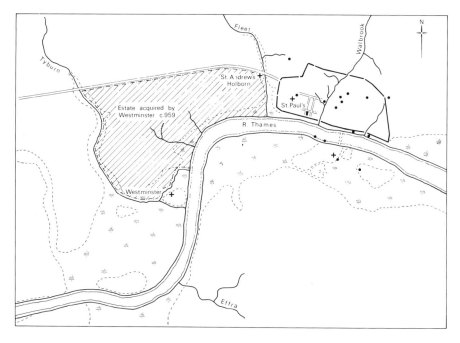

FIG. 14 Archaeological evidence for occupation in London in the late ninth to mid-tenth centuries. The only artefacts which can be reliably dated to this period are coins. The main elements of the Cheapside street grid date to this period and the position of the Bishop of Worcester's property is shown in black.

London. London was amongst the most important mints of England in the reign of Athelstan, in the second quarter of the tenth century, since it was decreed that eight moneyers could work there, at a time when most mints were limited to one. Only Canterbury and Winchester, the capitals of ninth-century Kent and Wessex, were allowed similar numbers. There are no charters referring to identifiable properties in London in the tenth century and so it is not possible to identify any features in London directly. Until recently it was thought that at least documents proved that the bridge had been rebuilt, since a woman accused of being a witch was taken to London Bridge. However, David Hill of the University of Manchester has questioned even this, since the document in which the Bridge is named is concerned with lands in Northamptonshire. He would see the London Bridge of the charter as a local bridge, named perhaps because it carried the London Road (Hill 1976). Even this is of great interest since it would show that London was seen as a major focal point in the road system at an early date.

The archaeological evidence from the city cannot yet be used to its fullest due, as explained above, to the difficulty in giving a close date to the most common find of the period, LSS ware. Coins of tenth-century date are rare. Only two have been found in recent excavations and neither is in a tenth-century context. One of these is from a building excavated on the site of the General Post Office Headquarters, Newgate Street, while the other was found at Billingsgate lorry park, but in what is probably an eleventh-century deposit.

Previous tenth-century coin finds are few but, interestingly, concentrate in the eastern half of the city, between Cornhill and Aldgate. They might suggest that the tenth-century settlement was concentrated along the main roads through the city as, indeed, seems to be the case in other late Saxon towns. However, excavation in this area has not revealed any concentration of early finds, so the pattern may be fortuitous.

Several pieces of timber, having been analysed by tree-ring specialists, have been shown to have been probably felled in the tenth century, although few can be dated to the year, or even within half a century for that matter. A group of such timbers were excavated in a pit at Milk Street, in the western half of the city, just north of Cheapside (*see* Fig. 15). They date the infilling of the pit to the second quarter of the tenth century or later. A similar date was obtained from a single timber from a drain alongside a building fronting onto Botolph Lane, in the eastern part of the city, to the south of Eastcheap. Both these results are tantalising. They show that timbers which could give an absolute date do survive in opposite ends of the city. Eventually, with luck, this type of analysis will show just how quickly the late Saxon city was settled but at present two extreme views are possible. First, that all parts of the city were occupied from at least the 880s, and that it rapidly took on its medieval character.

FIG. 15   A view of the 1976 excavation at Milk Street showing late Saxon and later pits
running in lines from the street frontage, presumably along the lines of property boundaries.
Fragments of oak from one of these pits were dated to the early tenth century by
dendrochronology. (Museum of London)

The other view is that all the archaeological evidence for tenth-century
activity in the city should be compressed into a short period at the end of
the century, perhaps the last third. Any further expansion or compression
would probably strain the evidence but both options are equally possible.

Pits containing LSS ware are often found orientated in the same direction,
and even in the same alignments, as later medieval pits. This is taken to
indicate that the properties which used them had the same boundaries as

their successors. Such a pattern, of narrow properties each with a building fronting onto the street and open ground and pits behind, is found in the early tenth century at sites such as Coppergate in York and Flaxengate in Lincoln. For this reason it is quite possible that the 'long chronology' for London is the correct one, although at the beginning of the tenth century both York and Lincoln were within the Viking-held Danelaw and no similar evidence yet exists from English-held towns. A recent study of the coin finds from London gives support to the 'short chronology', since it reveals a sudden increase in the number of coins lost, as well as hoards deposited, in the last two decades of the tenth century, although the increase in the number of moneyers at this time also suggests that there were more coins to be lost (*see* Fig. 16).

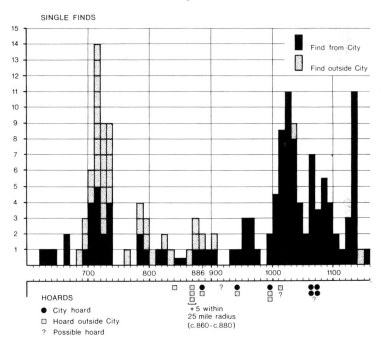

FIG. 16 Histogram showing finds of stray coins and hoards in the central London area. (Information supplied by Peter Stott, Museum of London.) This histogram does not directly reflect the period when coins were lost, since before 973 coins could have a long period of currency.

Outside the city walls there is little evidence for tenth-century occupation. A well which contained sherds of LSS ware was excavated at Hibernia Wharf in Southwark and similar sherds have been found on other sites at the northern end of the settlement, close to the waterfront. Excavations on properties fronting onto the main streets leading out of the city have so far shown little evidence that they were occupied during the tenth century. It seems that at this time one would have stepped into fields as soon as one walked out of Aldgate, Bishopsgate or Aldersgate. No excavations have taken place outside Newgate or Ludgate but the steep slope from there down to the Fleet is probably sufficient to guarantee that no levels survive, even if these roads were ever fronted by tenth-century buildings. Further out, on the other side of the Fleet, there is no evidence that any of the former trading settlement survived, although a church is known to have existed at St Andrew's Holborn. The nearest sites to have produced tenth-century finds are Westminster Abbey, which was refounded and re-endowed in the middle of the century, and the Treasury site. It would be important to know whether a shrunken settlement survived along the Whitehall/Strand/Fleet Street line. It is not actually known whether a road existed there at the time but this is, as stated before, the poorest area of archaeological survival in the whole of the Strand settlement.

Archaeological and historical sources agree that London was a thriving town in the early eleventh century (*see* Fig. 17). This is shown most clearly by the role which London played in the wars against the Vikings. In the late tenth century, Viking raiders once again started to menace the coasts of England. In 991 the port of Ipswich was harried by a group of Vikings under Olaf Tryggvason (later King of Norway). At the port of Maldon the Vikings won a battle against the English who agreed to pay tribute. In the following year it was decided to gather all the available

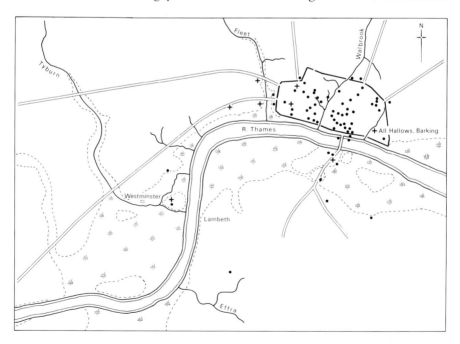

FIG. 17 Archaeological evidence for occupation in London in the tenth to early eleventh centuries. The majority of the finds marked on this map are potsherds which could be from as early as the late ninth or early tenth century but which were certainly in use no later than *c.* 1050.

ships at London and attempt to engage the enemy at sea, although this plan was foiled by the treachery of Ealdorman Eadric. Two years later London was attacked by a Viking force under the command of Olaf and Swein, King of Denmark. They are said in the *Anglo-Saxon Chronicle* to have had ninety-four ships and 'kept up an unceasing attack on the city, and they purposed, moreover, to set it on fire, but there they suffered greater loss and injury than ever thought possible that any garrison would inflict upon them. But on this day the holy Mother of God manifested her clemency to the garrison and delivered them from their foes' (ASC sa. 994; Whitelock 1968 No. 1, 214).

There is no doubt that the defences of the city were in good order and were being manned by a sizeable force. The garrison of no other fort in the whole of this long campaign (which lasted until 1014) is recorded as holding out against the Vikings, and many are known to have been sacked. In 1009 the remnant of the English fleet, which had been stationed at Sandwich, was brought back to London. Later that year the Vikings were based somewhere in the Thames, from where they made attacks on London 'but, praise be to God, she still stands safe and sound, and the Danes always suffered heavy losses there' (ASC sa. 1009; Whitelock 1968 No. 1, 220).

The Vikings then set off through the Chilterns to Oxford, which they burnt. In their absence levies were gathered at London, causing the Vikings on their return to avoid the city by crossing the Thames at Staines. Three years later London was again centre stage. Ealdorman Eadric and all the English council were in London while a tribute of £48,000 was gathered for the Danes. Aelfseah, archbishop of Canterbury, who was being held hostage by the Danes, was killed by drunken Danes who were angry that he would not allow a ransom to be paid for him. His body was taken by the citizens into London and buried in St Paul's. When the *Chronicle* entry was written, some time between 1012 and 1023, miracles were being reported at his tomb.

In 1013 the Danes' campaign was stepped up and an effort made to take over the whole kingdom. After sailing up the Trent to Gainsborough, Swein received the submission of the Northumbrians and all the shires north of Watling Street. He then took his forces south, ravaging the countryside as soon as they left the Danelaw. First Oxford and then Winchester surrendered, but the citizens of London 'would not submit, but held out against them with the utmost valour, because King Ethelred was inside, and Thurkil with him' (ASC sa. 1013; Whitelock 1968 No. 1, 223).

Thurkil was captain of a force of forty-five Viking ships which transferred their allegiance to the English king after the tribute of 1012. Swein did not attack London but turned westwards. At Bath the remaining parts of England submitted to him and he started back towards his ships which, together with the first hostages, had been left in the care of his son, Cnut.

At this point the citizens of London submitted. Ethelred and his family fled to France, where they stayed with Queen Emma's brother, Duke Richard of Normandy, but before Swein could consolidate his hold on the kingdom he died. His Viking companions chose Cnut to succeed him but the English council decided to recall Ethelred. It is clear from the *Chronicle* entry for 1016 that the king was based in London and was unsure of his support elsewhere in England. When Ethelred's son Edmund gathered levies to fight Cnut's army, which was harrying Warwickshire, they refused to fight without the king and the citizens of London. This prevarication continued throughout the year and while Edmund travelled throughout England, harrying those parts of the country which had submitted to Cnut while Cnut harried the rest, Ethelred stayed in London. On St George's Day he died and 'all the councillors who were in London, and the citizens, chose Edmund as king' (ASC sa. 1016; Whitelock 1968 No. 1, 226). By this date, evidently, the citizens of London themselves had become a powerful political force.

A fortnight later Cnut's fleet, which had presumably been based some-where in the Bristol Channel or Severn Valley, reached Greenwich and, finding their way up river blocked by the garrison manning London Bridge, dug a great channel to the south of the bridge, dragged their boats to the west and then built siegeworks around the city. Edmund managed to leave the city before this and made his way to Wessex, while the Viking army marched on London. Once again London held out and the Vikings moved off. Edmund was advised to come to terms with the Danes, which he did at Alney, in Gloucestershire. By this treaty Edmund held Wessex, and Cnut all England north of the Thames. London had to buy peace with the Danes, who once again took up winter quarters there with their ships. On 30th November, however, Edmund died and Cnut was chosen as king. He divided the kingdom into four earldoms, including Wessex and Mercia.

There is no evidence to suggest that London played as vital a role in the England of Cnut and his successors, Harold and Harthacnut, although on the death of Cnut it is recorded that his *litsmen*, his personal guard, were in London and were presumably based there. These men were a personal bodyguard and their presence in London may mean that London was Cnut's base. Be that as it may, his body was buried at Winchester, to join those of the kings of Wessex. His son, Harold, died in 1039 and was buried at Westminster, breaking the previous tradition, although his half-brother, Harthacnut, who died less than two years later, was buried at Winchester.

Despite the previous burial of Harold I at Westminster, it was Edward the Confessor who was responsible for the promotion of the abbey as part of a palace complex at Westminster (*see* Fig. 18). It has been suggested that Edward moved the royal palace out of the city to

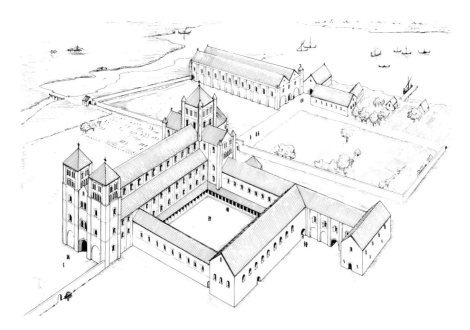

FIG. 18 An artist's reconstruction of Edward the Confessor's abbey, Westminster. Looking north-east towards the city of London. (After Terry Ball and Richard Gem)

Westminster and that the old palace site was used for the new college of St Martin le Grand. Ethelred must certainly have spent some time within the walls of the city, when it was under siege, and there are late traditions which located the royal palace in the region of the Cripplegate fort.

The archaeological evidence for London in the early eleventh century is more precise and more varied than that for the previous century. Excavations along the Saxon waterfront from the Thames Exchange site to Billingsgate lorry park have shown that there was some activity in front of the riverside wall, which was still standing. At New Fresh Wharf, next to the site of old London Bridge, a series of wooden stakes were set in rows in the foreshore (*see* Fig. 19). These may have been intended to keep a hard standing area in position or, it has been suggested, could have been part of a defence around London Bridge. The current view, however, is that they formed the base of a jetty. Parts of a timber boat were found stacked over the stakes in one place but it is doubted whether a similar covering existed everywhere. Samples of wood from the stakes were examined by dendrochronology but an absolute date could not be established. However, a relative date was obtained between one sample and another sample in the clay bank which overlay the stakes. The two trees were felled about sixty-five years apart but the calendar dates could not be established. Since the trees in the later structure were felled over a long period, from the late tenth century to *c.* 1020, the earlier tree could have

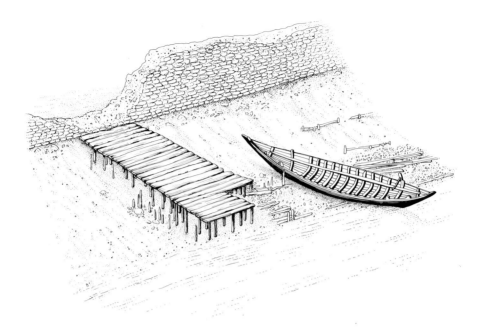

FIG. 19   An isometric reconstruction of the Thames foreshore at New Fresh Wharf in the early eleventh century. The Roman riverside wall must have been breached to allow access but the nature of the opening is complete supposition.

been felled in the early to mid-tenth century. The river silt buried underneath the boat timbers produced only Roman finds, which may mean that this structure represents the first use of the site since the Roman period. The succeeding clay bank was altogether more impressive. It consisted of a large clay bank with timber lacing and, probably, a timber facing, although if this is so it had been robbed in the late eleventh century.

At the Billingsgate lorry park site immediately to the east, the first late Saxon use of the waterfront was very similar to the clay bank from New Fresh Wharf and was erected over silt which contained only Roman finds. Timbers in the bank included a number felled in the same period, 1039/40. There was no evidence that the stakes found at New Fresh Wharf extended so far east and the general impression gained from these two excavations is that activity started in the west, closest to the bridge, and took perhaps fifty years to reach the Billingsgate site. From the mid-eleventh century onwards, however, the timber waterfronts were replaced at intervals of twenty to thirty years. Subsequent structures have been dated to *c.* 1055, *c.* 1080 or later and *c.* 1108 or later.

Billingsgate itself lay further east and is first recorded in a twelfth or thirteenth-century manuscript, attached to the fourth law code of Ethelred II. This manuscript undoubtedly had an eleventh-century prototype but cannot definitely be shown to pre-date the Danish conquest of 1016. It is concerned with the rights and dues of Londoners and must have been the result of an inquest not unlike that held by William I which gave rise to the Domesday Book. Apart from having the first record of the name Billingsgate, the document records Aldersgate and Cripplegate. It also names the origin of many of the traders in London and the regulations controlling them and is a mine of information about late Saxon London (*see* page 103).

Coins of the early to mid-eleventh century are much more frequent finds than those of the preceding century, although there are still only a handful from excavations, of which only two in particular may be useful for determining the absolute date of archaeological finds. One of these, a penny of Cnut, is from a pit excavated at Milk Street in 1976; another was found in 1959 in a pit underlying St Nicholas Acon Church. Several hoards of late tenth and early eleventh-century date must have been buried at the time of the Viking sieges of London while the absence of later hoards, until the Norman conquest, testifies to the relative security of London under the Danish kings and Edward the Confessor. The number of both loose coins and hoards of the early to mid-eleventh century show an intensification in the trade of London. It is also at this period that the first cut pennies are found in London, showing that coins were used for small change, not just for large transactions.

The evidence from the dated timbers and the stratified coins allows the pottery and other finds found with them to be dated too. From this, it is clear that LSS ware may have been current in 1039–40 but had certainly gone out of use by *c.* 1055. There are, however, new types of pottery, sandy wares, found with the shelly ware which must have come into use some time before. As a rough approximation it is probable that they were current between *c.* 1000 and *c.* 1050. It is therefore possible to date any feature containing freshly broken sherds of LSS ware to the early to mid-eleventh century or ealier, and if it also contains the sandy wares it is possible to say that it is of eleventh rather than tenth-century date. From this we can determine which parts of the city were occupied by *c.* 1050 (*see* Fig. 17), what type of artefacts were in use, what types of pit were used and what buildings were being lived in.

Fragments of over forty buildings of this period have been excavated in the walled city and these can be divided into those which were built at ground level and fronted onto the contemporary streets and those with timber cellars or half-cellars, most of which were found at the backs of properties. In many cases the buildings themselves do not survive but their likely position can be shown by the fact that there is a strip of land at the frontage which is not cut into by late Saxon pits (*see* Fig. 20). At Milk Street, however, pits seem to have been dug in lines along the boundary between one property and the next. This presumably means that there were thin strips of undeveloped land in between the buildings, since at that site traces were found of a ground level building which would have fronted onto the street. The pits which make up these lines range in date from the tenth or early eleventh century through to the twelfth century and suggest that the pattern of properties running back perpendicular to the streets had come into existence by the early to mid-eleventh century. The excavations at Botolph Lane did not produce evidence for the divisions between properties but did show that the earliest houses built on the site fronted onto Botolph Lane.

By the middle of the eleventh century there is abundant archaeological evidence to show that a large settlement had grown up inside the walled

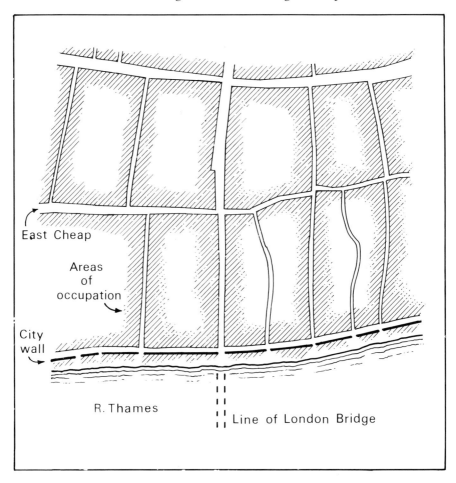

FIG. 20 A hypothetical model of settlement north of London Bridge in the later tenth or eleventh century. The minor lanes, Pudding Lane and Lovat Lane, would have provided access to the backs of properties fronting the main streets as well as linking Eastcheap with the waterfront via gates in the riverside wall. It is not known whether a precursor to Thames Street ran behind the Roman wall or whether, as in the western half of the waterfront, Thames Street was constructed when the wall was demolished.

city, although there were still many areas within the walls which were unoccupied. There is also evidence that the mid-eleventh-century town had a busy waterfront in front of the riverside wall. The archaeological evidence for the use of this waterfront consists of waterside structures and sherds of imported pottery. The latter occur throughout the town but, like the evidence from the waterfront itself, are mainly datable to the middle of the century and later. Both these lines of evidence suggest that late Saxon London grew to a considerable size before it again became an international port.

Outside the walls there is evidence for settlement at Southwark and in the Whitehall area to the north of Westminster. The site of the former mid-Saxon settlement was probably unoccupied. The church of St Andrew at Holborn must have served an agricultural community at this time and was probably founded during the life of *Lundenwic*.

4 Norman London

The citizens of London played an important role in the Norman conquest. Edward the Confessor died in 1066 and was buried in his newly-built church at Westminster. Since Edward had no son, the council chose Earl Harold of Wessex as their king. They were apparently carrying out the wish of Edward, although William of Normandy claimed that the crown had been promised to him and that Harold had taken an oath of allegiance to him. The Norwegians also had a long-standing claim to the English throne, through Cnut's conquest, and the first task for King Harold II was to confront a fleet of 300 ships under Harald Hardrada, King of Norway, which had landed on the Ouse, near York. Having marched north and defeated the Norwegians at the Battle of Stamford Bridge, word came to Harold that the Normans under Duke William had landed on the south coast. The exhausted English then marched south, via London, to their defeat and Harold's death at Hastings. The English survivors fled north. An early twelfth-century source tells how one leader, Ansgar the Staller, possibly the Sheriff of London, organised the defence of the city, although he was too wounded to walk.

William's army slowly marched towards London but upon reaching the Thames and finding their way across the bridge barred they headed west, ravaging the countryside as they went. Crossing the Thames at Wallingford, the Normans continued to keep a safe distance away from London while encircling it. When they reached Berkhamstead (Hertfordshire) they were met by a party from London offering the submission of the city. Despite this, one can follow the route of William's army by the trail of destruction which it caused between Berkhamstead and London. Soon after completing the conquest, William issued a charter to the Bishop, Sheriff and citizens of London, in which he promised them the same treatment under the law as they had enjoyed under Edward. Harold was regarded by the Normans as an usurper so they refused to acknowledge his reign. It is notable that the leading families in London in the late eleventh century were still English, whereas English landholders in the Middlesex and Surrey countryside had been almost totally replaced by Normans or other foreigners.

London was by no means free of Norman domination, however, and the most clear signs of the subjection of the city were the presence of castles – the White Tower in the south-east and Baynard's Castle and

Montfichet Tower in the south-west. The latter was regarded as a separate castle by William Fitzstephen in the late twelfth century but may have been part of the same complex as Baynard's Castle. The western castle(s) would have overshadowed the routeway from Westminster to the city, as well as being close to St Paul's and the mouth of the Fleet. The castle occupied a large part of this quarter of the city until the thirteenth century, by which time it was ruinous enough to allow the Blackfriars to obtain its former site and demolish both the castle and a stretch of the city wall to build their friary (*see* Fig. 21).

The Tower of London, on the other hand, was no temporary fortification (*see* Fig. 22) and continued to grow in line with developments in siege warfare until it formed a virtually impregnable castle under Edward III. William built the White Tower both as a fortress and a palace but also, one imagines, as a physical reminder to the citizens of London as to who held power in England. As the defences around the Tower grew, Londoners cannot have failed to notice that the area most heavily defended and most quickly modernised faced inwards to the city, rather than that looking east or south, where foreign attack might be expected.

FIG. 21 The ditch of Montfichet Tower, revealed during excavations in Carter Lane. (Museum of London)

FIG. 22   A reconstruction of the White Tower in the late eleventh century. The Roman city wall is in the foreground. (Museum of London)

It is possible, given these political circumstances, that it is in the immediately post-conquest period that London lost its southern defence. The riverside wall was almost certainly still standing at the time of the conquest. Without it, it is difficult to see why William could not have forced his way into the city from Southwark. In the *Carmen de Hastingae Proelio*, written *c*. 1125–40, London was said to have been 'protected on the left side by walls, on the right side by the river' (Morton and Muntz 1972, 40–1; Davis 1978). This suggests that the wall had receded from memory by the middle of the twelfth century, pointing to a demolition date in the late eleventh century. By *c*. 1174, when Fitzstephen wrote his description of London, the riverside wall was only a memory, having been washed away by the Thames. Excavations along the waterfront in the extreme south-west of the city showed that although the front face of the wall had been eroded and undercut by the river this could not account for large parts of the wall being found tipped northwards, towards the city, and immediately underlying the first surfaces of Upper Thames Street (*see* Fig. 23). Undoubtedly this section of the wall was deliberately demolished and a road constructed over it. Slightly to the east, where the stump of the Roman wall was found *in situ*, the surfaces of Upper Thames Street lay on top of it and a reclamation dump to the south. All these events can be dated by pottery found in the dumps and road make-ups to the late eleventh or early twelfth centuries. Similar pottery was found in the Billingsgate excavation associated with structures dated to *c*. 1080 and later.

It may, however, be too fanciful to imagine that the riverside wall was demolished to stop the citizens of London from defending their city, since other evidence shows that it was at this time that pressure of space within the walls finally built up to a point where the city spilt outside them. London is unfortunately absent from the Domesday Book, although blank pages left at the beginning of the Middlesex entry show that an entry had been intended. The surrounding estates were included but unfortunately they were grouped into two large manors, that of the Bishop of London centred on Stepney and that of the Abbot of Westminster, between Oxford Street and the Thames. The manor of Stepney virtually encircled the city and thus it is not possible to tell how many of the people who are recorded in that manor were truly rural peasants and how many actually lived in suburbs of London. However, in one instance a group of peasants are recorded as living outside the bishop's gate, which must be Bishopsgate. The boundary of the city at this point extends northwards, along the road, and it is tempting to think that this might actually represent the limit of settlement at the time when the boundary became fixed. Excavations at Stothard Place, 500 metres north of the city

Fig. 23   The riverside wall as found at Baynard's Castle in 1974. The wall was toppled northwards to form the foundation for Thames Street in the late eleventh or early twelfth century. Looking east, with half-metre scale. (Museum of London)

wall on Bishopsgate, have shown that the site was unoccupied until the late eleventh to early twelfth century, which would imply that the settlement recorded in Domesday Book was post-conquest. This may explain why the Domesday entry for this estate was dealt with anomalously.

A similar bulge occurs in the city boundary outside Aldersgate and, to a lesser extent, Cripplegate (*see* Fig. 24). Excavations on properties fronting onto the road leading north from Aldersgate have shown that there was no settlement anywhere along the street before *c.* 1050, since there is very little LSS ware from any of the sites. Just how soon after *c.* 1050 properties were occupied is difficult to tell from pottery but one site, just outside the city ditch at Aldersgate, produced a lead 'coin' stamped with the dies of Edward the Confessor which, although unstratified, is likely to have been disturbed from the fill of a large mid to late eleventh-century cess-pit. Similar evidence has been found all along the street as far as the junction with Carthusian Street, *c.* 400 metres north of the city wall.

Excavations along the roads leading to Cripplegate have been much less extensive than those along Bishopsgate and Aldersgate. Much was destroyed during the construction of the Barbican Centre without any archaeological record being made, but a small excavation just outside the gate carried out by Professor Grimes did produce evidence for timber buildings dating to the mid-eleventh century or later. The church of St Giles is said to have

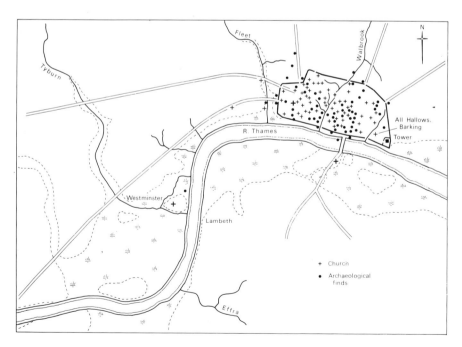

FIG. 24   Archaeological evidence for occupation in London in the late eleventh century. The finds are a mixture of coins and potsherds. Churches are marked as crosses. The apparent absence of settlement in Southwark is due to the relevant data not being available.

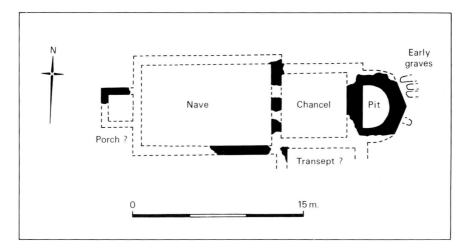

FIG. 25 The first stone church of St Bride's, Fleet Street, as revealed by excavation (after Grimes). Since the apse cut through earlier burials there must have been an earlier church on the site. The pit within the apse contained a sherd of eleventh-century pottery and this is the probable date of the stone church.

been founded *c.* 1090 by Alfhune, who became the first Hospitaler of St Bartholomew's Hospital in the early twelfth century. Cripplegate itself was mentioned in Ethelred the Unready's fourth law code and is also mentioned in a charter of William I of 1068. The spelling used for the name is the same in both cases, 'Crepelesgate', which would favour it being named after a person called Crepel. This is not a recorded Anglo-Saxon name, however, and the most likely derivation is from crepel meaning 'a hollow'. In William's charter the gate is referred to as a postern, emphasising its minor character, while excavations underneath and alongside Wood Street have recently shown that the street probably originally came to an end about 150 metres north of Cheapside but was extended to lead out of Cripplegate sometime after *c.* 1050.

Excavation along Fleet Street and the Strand has not so far been able to determine whether occupation continued along the street frontages from the mid-Saxon period onwards or whether there was a break. Excavations at St Bride's church did not provide conclusive dating evidence, although they suggest that the apsidal-ended stone church found by Professor Grimes might be quite late, since a shaft dug within the apse contained a sherd of eleventh-century pottery (*see* Fig. 25). Excavations to the south and east of St Bride's, well away from Fleet Street, have shown that much of this area was inundated by the Thames at an unknown date and only reclaimed in the fifteenth century. The presence of a fragment of timber on one site at Tudor Street dated to the tenth century cannot be interpreted since it was discovered after the excavation had finished when earth-moving machines had revealed a number of piles cutting through natural deposits. Excavations on the site of the City of London Boys School, south of Tudor Street, did, however, show that part of this area had been reclaimed in the late eleventh to early twelfth century.

Further west, a cluster of churches — St Dunstan, St Mary and St Clement Danes — were probably in existence in the eleventh century and may represent the shrunken Aldwych settlement or a new ribbon development, like those along Aldersgate and Bishopsgate. The dedication of the latter church, and the occasional use of the term 'Denchmans Street' for part of the Strand in the medieval period, led Sir Mortimer Wheeler to identify this area as the site of a Danish enclave, possibly a rich suburb strung out along the route from Westminster to the walled city. Certainly, this was the type of settlement seen in the area in the high medieval period, but to date no suitable sites have been available to excavate to test Wheeler's theory.

This expansion also affected some areas within the walled city. Excavations on sites in the Walbrook valley have shown that there was little human activity in the area until the late eleventh or early twelfth century. At Cross Keys Court, south of London Wall, a ditch was found cutting through and draining a natural marsh deposit which built up on the site some time after the fourth century. This ditch was filled with a spread of occupation debris, including scraps of leather waste. This deposit also filled four wattle-lined pits cut into a Roman road which, although by then covered by marsh, may have still acted as a causeway through the valley and been visible as drier land.

Similar evidence has been found on a site which is now part of the Central Criminal Court, Old Bailey. This area might have been expected to have been occupied quite early, perhaps even in the mid-Saxon period, since it is so close to St Paul's and the two gates. The excavation by Peter Marsden showed, however, that the majority of the pits on the site had been filled in the late eleventh to early twelfth century or later. It may be that the site was too close to the city wall for early occupation. It would have been important to maintain an open area, and probably an intra-mural road, behind the wall while it was in use as a military structure. The evidence from the Central Criminal Court site is therefore capable of the same two interpretations as that from the site of the riverside wall. By the eleventh century, the defence of the city, for whatever reason, was being treated as less important than the need for more space for housing.

The evidence for the churches of London will be examined later but seems to bear out the pattern found by archaeology, since a case has been made by Professor Brooke for the five churches placed just outside London's gates being of late eleventh or early twelfth-century date. The siting of a series of priories and other religious establishments around the edge of the city in the early twelfth century seems to confirm the pattern of suburban development described above (*see* Fig. 26). In 1123, St Bartholomew's

Hospital and Priory were squeezed into the space between the market of Smithfield and housing along Aldersgate. The Knights Templar originally had their headquarters on the other side of the Fleet valley, at Holborn, while another priory was situated at the south end of London Bridge in Southwark. Only in one case was it possible to find space within the walls, at Holy Trinity Priory just inside Aldgate. It may therefore be significant that there is no corresponding bulge in the city boundary outside of Aldgate, suggesting that development along Aldgate High Street was later or on a smaller scale than that along the other routes.

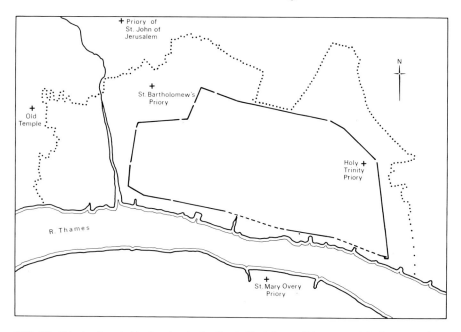

FIG. 26   Priories founded in London in the first half of the twelfth century. The location of these religious houses was governed by the built-up area. By *c.* 1100 therefore the city had outgrown its defences to the west and north-west but was still relatively empty to the east, allowing Holy Trinity Priory to be built within the walls.

The changes which we can see between London in the middle of the eleventh century and in the following century are slight. On many sites within the town occupation continued without any observable interruption. The erection of the White Tower and Baynard's Castle obviously caused some dislocation to Londoners. The White Tower must certainly have had an effect on the whole of the south-eastern quarter of the city. Although as yet undated, it is likely that Tower Street was constructed soon after the foundation of the White Tower in order to link the castle with Eastcheap. Elsewhere the main impression of the first century of Norman rule was of steady growth outside the city gates and in particular in front of, and eventually over the line of, the demolished riverside wall.

Summary

In Part One we have seen how London continued to be an important centre for the administration of the diocese of Britain to the end of the fourth century. At that time, before there is any convincing evidence for Anglo-Saxon settlement in the area, the city went into an abrupt decline. We may never know whether it was completely abandoned and it may have formed the stronghold for a British ruler for a generation or two. By the late fifth century, however, London was surrounded by Anglo-Saxon settlements and it is difficult to believe that it could have been occupied at all without a scatter of early Anglo-Saxon finds being lost within its walls. There then followed a century during which we have no evidence at all for human activity in or around the walled city. When London was chosen in 604 as the site of the cathedral there may have been small existing settlements both within the walls and in the Charing Cross area, but the evidence is by no means definite.

Later in the seventh century there is no doubt that a *wic* existed along the Strand, and this *wic* grew during the eighth and into the ninth century. It is likely that it survived Viking attacks in 841 and 851 but there is no further documentary or archaeological evidence for its continued existence after the Viking raid of 871. In 886 London was occupied by King Alfred and by 889, only three years later, the town had been relocated within the walled city. Archaeological evidence is not yet able to shed more light on this movement and seems to indicate that the initial settlement was relatively small. During the tenth century the town inside the walls grew and by the end of the century there is evidence for activity on parts of the waterfront close to London Bridge. By the middle of the eleventh century this waterfront activity had grown and may have been continuous on either side of the bridge between Dowgate and Billingsgate. This century is marked historically by the Norman conquest and archaeologically by the construction of castles within the walls. These castles had an effect on settlement within the walls, but the main change in settlement was the spread of occupation both within the walls and outside the gates.

Part Two

Aspects of
Saxon London

In this part of the book, certain themes which have already been summarised in Part One are examined in more detail. The top of the social scale is explored by looking at political control over the London area, its nature and how it changed through the period. This leads inevitably to a consideration of the Church, whose organisation and history mirrors that of the secular state. The role of London as a place of defence and strategic importance is then examined, followed by an essay on trade and particularly the contribution of archaeology to the study of London's trade. This then leads to a summary of the evidence for London's mint, its road system and the countryside surrounding the town. The comments here have been restricted mainly to the area of historic Middlesex, although London's success or otherwise must have affected Surrey in a similar manner. The evidence for daily life in Saxon London is then briefly surveyed, an aspect recently covered in detail elsewhere (Horsman, Milne and Milne 1988; Vince 1989). Finally, an assessment of how London compares with other English towns in the Saxon period is made and some areas are suggested where it hoped that archaeology is in a position to clarify our present understanding of London's development.

5 Administration

The image of a medieval kingdom, with the king and his courtiers in his castle overlooking his town, is so deeply ingrained into our popular culture that it is difficult to stand back and think why there should be a connection between a town and royalty and whether it has always been the case.

First, it is important to remember that the London area is likely to have undergone some drastic changes in government between the fourth and the eleventh centuries. In the fourth century London was a part of the Roman Empire. At that time the Empire was organised into *civitates*, regions administered from a capital city and divided into *vici* and *pagus* which can be roughly thought of as urban and rural districts from which taxes (both in cash and kind) were extracted. The tax would partly pay for the administration of the *civitas* and the army and part would be sent back to Rome. London itself in the late fourth century was the seat of the *vicarius* of Britain, a diocese which consisted of four or five provinces – *Maxima Caesariensis, Flavia Caesariensis, Britannia Prima, Britannia Secunda* and, possibly, *Valentia*. There is a view that Valentia is merely a re-naming of an existing province. London is thought to have been the capital of *Maxima Caesariensis*. From its geographical position it is very likely that it would have been the seat of officials dealing with the administration of the *civitates* of St Albans, Chichester, Canterbury and, possibly, Silchester (on the border of Hampshire and Berkshire). In the early fifth century there is evidence, in the form of a letter from the Emperor Honorius to the *civitates* of Britain, that although the *civitates* still survived the Roman administration did not. If there had been a vicar of Britain, Honorius would probably have written to him instead. St Germanus of Auxerre visited Britain in 429 in order to combat the influence of Pelagius, a monk who denied the doctrine of original sin, on the Christian community. The only place in Britain that Germanus visited which can be identified is Verulamium, since he was shown the shrine of St Alban. It is possible, therefore, that within the *civitas* of the Catuvellauni, which included both Verulamium and London, the *civitas* was administered from the former while the latter was concerned solely with the administration of the diocese.

It may therefore be in Verulamium that we should be seeking the headquarters of the British rulers of the London area in the early fifth century. From the excavations conducted there by Professor Frere, then at the Oxford Institute of Archaeology, we know that many aspects of Roman life which had disappeared elsewhere continued in Verulamium. These included building in stone with courses of tile and the provision of a piped water supply (Frere 1983, 24–5).

Not enough is known of the actual events of the early fifth century to use them to suggest what role London might have had at that time. The city itself seems to have been substantially deserted at the end of the fourth century but it is quite possible for a much reduced presence to have lingered on. All that can be said at present is that there is not a shred of evidence on any of the sites excavated in the city for the presence of people living in the city in the early fifth century. The Billingsgate bath-house brooch (*see* Fig. 27) is the only artefact found which was actually made in the fifth century, and that came from a context which emphasises the deserted nature of the city. Most likely the lower Thames valley formed a zone given over to Anglo-Saxon settlers in return for the defence of the coast, but the very fact that it was used as a refuge for the British after the battle of Crecganford in 457 shows that there was not a Germanic garrison within the walled city.

To the north of London, centred on the Chilterns, a British kingdom seems to have survived until the late sixth century since the Anglo-Saxons fought against the British at a number of places along the foot of the

FIG. 27 A fifth-century brooch found in the ruins of Billingsgate bathhouse. (Museum of London)

Chiltern scarp (ASC sa. 571; Whitelock 1968 No. 1, 146). The boundary of this kingdom is not known but Grim's Dyke, a post-Roman bank and ditch in Stanmore in north Middlesex, may show that it roughly followed the later boundary between Hertfordshire and Middlesex (*see* Fig. 28). Wheeler interpreted this dyke as part of the defences of a British kingdom centred on London, since the defended area is to the south of the dyke (Wheeler 1935, 59–73), while a section through the dyke at Pear Tree Wood certainly shows that it contains a substantial quantity of later Roman artefacts (Castle 1975, 270–3). At an unknown date in the sixth century this British enclave fell to the Anglo-Saxons and by the early seventh century was part of the kingdom of the East Saxons.

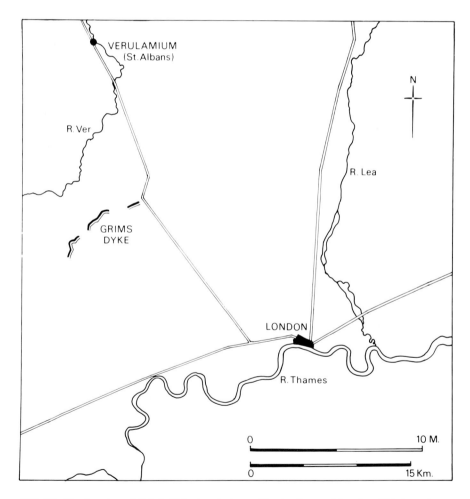

FIG. 28   The location of Grim's Dyke in relation to Verulamium and London. This boundary was definitely in existence in the pre-Roman Iron Age but the eastern stretch, overlooking Watling Street, was constructed in the late Roman period or later.

We know from Bede's account of the introduction of Christianity into the London area in the early seventh century that London was the *metropolis* of the kings of the East Saxons. From genealogies it is possible to show that the East Saxon dynasty probably came into existence in the mid to late sixth century, probably under the protection of the kings of Kent (York 1985, 16). From *c.* 616 onwards we know of more than one East Saxon king ruling at the same time and it is likely that the East Saxon kingdom was, like Northumbria and Wessex, a confederation of provinces each of which retained its own administration.

Sometimes a single king would have power over all districts and some-times power would be split between them. If this is the case then the district containing London would have existed as a separate entity by the early seventh century. Unfortunately by *c.* 700, when we have a small amount of documentary evidence for the spheres of influence of the co-rulers of Essex, there is no support for this theory. Swafred granted land in both Middlesex and Essex while his co-ruler Sigeheard confirmed a grant to Barking Abbey in Essex but also confirmed a grant of land at Fulham in Middlesex. The Middle Saxon province could either have been created to increase the efficiency of administration, or as a result of the partition of the kingdom on the death of Saberht in *c.* 616, or it might originally have been a separate kingdom which was annexed by the East Saxon kings some time between the foundation of their kingdom in *c.* 550 and the foundation of the bishopric in 604. The name of the province is not recorded by Bede but is recorded as that of the Middle Saxons in a charter of 704 granting land at Twickenham to Bishop Waldhere of London. This name would have been particularly apposite during the late sixth to mid-seventh centuries when the West Saxons held the land to the west of the Chilterns and the East Saxons held the land to the east. After the West Saxons lost control of what later became Oxfordshire and Buckinghamshire the giving of the name 'Middle Saxons' would have been archaic, although John Blair has suggested that the Middle Saxon kingdom existed briefly in the late seventh century (Blair, 1989).

Place-names preserve the names of peoples within the province – Yeading (Geddi's people) or Ealing (Gilla's people) and in the old name for Harrow, Hergae Gumeningas (the sanctuary of Gumen's people). The territory of these groups is unknown but cannot have been more than a few later medieval parishes. It could have been considerably less, approximating to the administrative units which bore those names in the tenth century and later. Some of these names occur in seventh-century charters but it is unclear whether these groups were still distinct entities by the seventh century or whether they had merely given their name to a block of land. How much authority Gumen, Geddi or Gilla had is not known, but they probably belonged to the upper class of Anglo-Saxon society whose rights and duties were recorded in writing in the late seventh century by the kings of Kent and Wessex (Bailey, 1989).

The limited toponymic and documentary sources show that London would have come under the control of increasingly powerful rulers during the sixth and seventh centuries. Bede's account of the foundation of St Paul's makes it clear that King Aethelerht of Kent, in his position as Bretwalda or 'over-king', had considerable sway in the territory of the East Saxons. Aethelbald's successor Eadbald, who reigned from 616 to 640, may have issued a gold coin bearing both his name and that of London (Sutherland 1940, Nos. 77, Pl. IV no. 22). A coin in the Crondall (Hampshire) hoard shared the same obverse but the reverse does not mention London. If so, this is remarkable for three reasons. First, few other Anglo-Saxon coins bear the king's name until the reign of Offa in the late eighth century. Second, this coin would be amongst the earliest minted in England, and third, it is evidence for strong Kentish influence in the East Saxon kingdom after the expulsion of Bishop Mellitus and the reversion of the kingdom to paganism in 616.

A unique coin is too flimsy a piece of evidence to postulate any permanent royal establishment in London, although there may well have been one. A few decades later gold coins were certainly being minted there, but bear the name of the city without the name of the issuing authority (*see* page 110). Where the London mint would have been and how many moneyers it would have had are unknown. Later in the seventh century the laws of Hlothere of Kent show that he had a hall in London where Kentish merchants were to register their transactions. Such a hall would presumably have been a large timber building of a class now known from several sites (such as Northampton and Cheddar) and which are collectively known to archaeologists as 'palaces'. There may have been a single king's hall in London, successively controlled by the kings of Mercia, Kent and Wessex as the overlordship of London changed during the seventh to ninth centuries, but it is equally possible that London boasted several such halls. A recent analogy might be the far eastern trading stations of the eighteenth and early nineteenth centuries where rows of huts might be seen, each sporting the flag of a different European power.

Anglo-Saxon kings in the seventh to ninth centuries did not have a single residence but moved around the country from district to district. The purpose of such a peripatetic existence was partly to solve the problem of how to consume the rent in kind owed to the king without moving vast quantities of perishable foodstuffs around the country. At intervals a council or *witan* would be held, policy decided and such matters as the transfer of land ratified. From surviving charters we know that the kings of Mercia held councils at London but were more often to be found at Chelsea.

There is a tradition that the king's palace lay just within the city walls, on the site of the Cripplegate fort (*see* Fig. 29). The best evidence for this

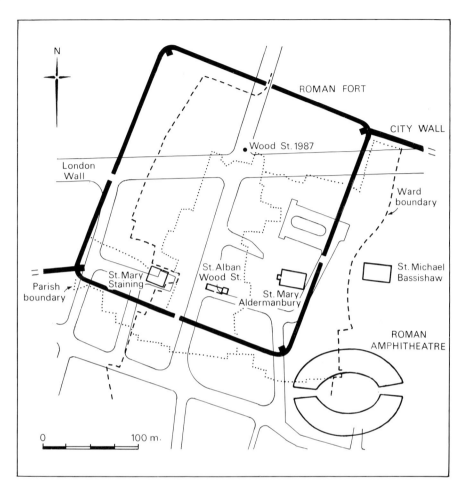

FIG. 29 The Cripplegate fort area, showing the location of St Alban, Wood Street and Aldermanbury (immediately to the north of St Mary Aldermanbury). Note that neither the ward nor the parish boundaries respect the south or east walls of the Roman fort and that Wood Street runs over the south wall, rather than running through the south gate, but exits from the city through the north gate, Cripplegate itself. (Museum of London)

comes from a late eleventh-century source quoted by Mathew Paris in the early thirteenth century. It states that the liberties of the old royal palace then lay with a 'small house' which Dyson and Schofield identify as being on a tenement known as Aldermanbury (Dyson and Schofield 1984, 308). Further evidence to show that the palace lay within the walls comes from Florence of Worcester in his annal for 1017:

> And at the Lord's Nativity, when he [Cnut] was in London, he gave orders for the perfidious ealdorman Eadric to be killed in the palace, because he feared to be at some time deceived by his treachery, as his

former lords Ethelred and Edmund had frequently been deceived; and he ordered his body to be thrown over the wall of the city and left unburied (Whitelock 1968, No. 9, 186).

From the time of Ethelred onwards every king spent some time in London, often using it as his main base. The evidence for an earlier royal palace within the walled city is much less certain. It may, for example, be mere coincidence that the church of St Alban Wood Street does lie on the north-south axial road to the south of the centre of the Roman Cripplegate fort. Unfortunately, excavations on the site of the church following its destruction in the Blitz were inconclusive and there is no reason to date the small stone church discovered beneath the medieval foundations to any period earlier than the eleventh century. Nevertheless, by the middle of the sixteenth century there was a tradition that this church had once been the chapel of King Offa's palace. Aldermanbury lies over the site of the east gate tower of the fort (Dyson and Schofield 1981, 61–3). The survival of a Roman gate tower and its subsequent reuse as a fortification or prestige accommodation is certainly known elsewhere. It is unfortunate, however, that there is no evidence from archaeology either way. We are even unsure whether the southern or eastern walls of the fort survived above ground after its northern and western walls were incorporated into the Roman city wall. The recently-discovered amphitheatre at Guildhall Yard would also have made an ideal site for a post-Roman royal centre. On the Continent such reuse of amphitheatres during the Merovingian period is well-attested, although the evidence from Britain is much less positive. The Guildhall Yard excavations conclusively showed that the stone walls and the arena within were covered with a fourth-century 'dark earth' dump and the site seems to have lain empty until the late eleventh century. Nevertheless, the outline of the amphitheatre was followed by two medieval streets, Aldermanbury and Basinghall Street, and it is possible that the site was marked in the post-Roman period by some major topographic features, most likely tributaries of the Walbrook.

It was at Chelsea, rather than London, that King Alfred held his council to plan the restoration of London. He allocated blocks of land within the walled city to the Bishop of Worcester and the Archbishop of Canterbury and may well have given similar blocks to lay lords. We do not know the internal organisation of these properties. They may have been small versions of a rural estate, with hall, chapel and ancillary buildings, or they may have been subdivided and let to artisans and merchants. The king may have kept some properties for his own use and there are indications in the late tenth and eleventh centuries that the king sometimes dwelt in London. We know that Ethelred II was besieged in London (*see* page 31) but that was an exceptional circumstance. Place-names record Aetheling Street (Aetheling being an Anglo-Saxon name for prince) and

Aldermanbury, the defended enclosure, or manor, of the Ealdorman (a regional ruler whose duties were taken over by the earls after Cnut's conquest). The presence of Cnut's *litsmen*, his personal guard, in London at his death may be taken as evidence that he had a base in the city (*see* page 32) while later in the eleventh century there is circumstantial evidence that the king held a block of land to the north of the cathedral, just inside Aldersgate, since that area was acquired by the college of St Martin-le-Grand. The reason for the foundation of the college may be that the land was no longer required by the king, Edward the Confessor, who had decided to create a royal complex at Westminster.

Edward refounded the abbey at Westminster partly as his mausoleum (Gem 1986, 12–13). In 1066, a few days after the dedication of the abbey church, Edward died and was buried there. However, he was not the first English king to do so, since Harold I had been buried there in 1039 (*see* pages 32 and 63). Edward's probable ideal, that of the establishment of a dynastic mausoleum and cult centre at Westminster, was dashed by the Norman conquest but was ultimately revived by Henry III, who opened Edward's tomb and reburied his remains in a remarkable shrine of Italian workmanship.

Even in Harold II's short reign, London played an important part in royal life and seems to have been the base for the fleet. Harold's connection with Waltham Abbey, of which he was patron, confirms that he had personal interest in the London area. William I certainly seems to have treated Londoners with caution. The capitulation of the citizens of London marked the end of the conquest of England. William moved the royal treasury from Winchester to Westminster, where it was based in the Pyx Chapel in the abbey. Westminster was also, with Winchester and Gloucester, a place where the king celebrated the major religious festivals, held his Great Councils and symbolically wore the crown (Stenton 1971, 631, 641).

William I can be seen to have been following an English precedent in his dealings with London. By the end of the tenth century the town had become so large and prosperous that its inhabitants had become a political force. Their progress towards self-government is described in detail by Professor Brooke (Brooke and Keir 1975, 185–232). Royalty became locked into a complex relationship with the city, needing the support of the citizens but fearing their power. Nevertheless, it should not be forgotten that London was not the capital of England at this time. Surely and steadily throughout the twelfth and thirteenth centuries it continued to grow in size and importance, and just as surely the twin royal centres at Westminster and the Tower of London grew too.

6 The Church

By the end of the fourth century the majority of the population of London may have been Christian. Inhumation cemeteries outside the walls of towns such as Dorchester in Dorset, Winchester and London itself have been excavated and show that whereas the dead were sometimes buried with their possessions in graves aligned in any direction (but often north-south), the later fourth-century graves were usually laid east-west with few if any gravegoods. Hobnails and jewellery show that the dead were buried clothed but otherwised unaccompanied. At St Bartholomew's Hospital, London, a small area of the Smithfield cemetery was excavated. Orderly burials, one upon the other, show that it had been used intensively. Archaeological evidence for the latest use of this cemetery is, understandably, rare but a buckle found at Smithfield in the nineteenth century probably dates to the very end of the fourth or early in the fifth century (*see* Fig. 30). Similar late burials have been found in the cemetery flanking Bishopsgate, at Stothard Place for example.

FIG. 30   A late fourth or early fifth-century belt buckle from Smithfield. (British Museum)

Churches would have been built to serve this community. Pagan temples lost their official support early in the fourth century and those in London must surely have declined. Evidence for the abandonment of religious precincts in other towns during the fourth century can be found. At Verulamium, for example, the theatre, which was attached to a temple complex, was used as a rubbish dump during the late fourth century, starting *c*. 390 (Frere 1983, 21 and fn. 2), while at Bath the temple of Sulis-Minerva went into decline at about the same time (Cunliffe 1985, 74−5), although the sacred spring was still being visited in the early fifth century. Some temples may have been converted to churches, while the Mithraeum on the bank of the Walbrook seems to have been sacked during the fourth century, possibly by Christians (Grimes 1986, 3). Nevertheless, the Mithraeum continued in use later and Mithraic sculptures and a statue of Bacchus were found in rubble from its final, undated, destruction.

Despite the certain presence of a bishop in London by 314, when he attended the Council of Arles, there is no archaeological evidence yet for the location of his or any other church. In Lincoln, whose bishop also attended the Arles council, the foundations of an apsed timber building in the centre of the forum courtyard must surely belong to a church. The site seems to have been a religious focus throughout the Saxon period and eventually became the site of the parish church of St Paul in the Bail. This church may, however, date to the fifth or even sixth century since the only dating evidence is that it was robbed before some burials in a cemetery of fifth to seventh-century date were interred. The forum courtyard in London was investigated in 1977 in the Gracechurch Street tunnel, which ran north-south down the centre of the forum. Above the initial gravel surfaces was a deposit of silt, interpreted either as an ornamental pond or a marsh which formed in the courtyard after the Roman period, owing to the fact that the courtyard was at a lower level than the surrounding land (Marsden 1987, 67−70).

The basilica to the north of the forum would not only have formed a suitable location for a church, but is also the site of the medieval church of St Peter Cornhill. Tradition asserts that it is the site of the Roman church. Excavation in the area around it has shown that the medieval and later building sits on top of an aisle of the basilica. Cornhill itself crosses the north-west corner of the basilica and may well be a pre-Alfredian road (*see* page 123). The west end of the basilica therefore fell down before the end of the ninth century but it is quite possible that fragments of its walls which were standing were incorporated into a church. Similar suggestions have been made to account for the survival of standing Roman masonry at Wroxeter, Leicester and Lincoln. Sir Mortimer Wheeler took this hypothesis seriously in 1935 and suggested that this was the reason why St Paul's had been founded on the crest of the western hill of London, as an Anglo-Saxon counterpart to the pre-existing, British, St Peter's on the east hill. There is, however, absolutely no evidence from the numerous excavations in the area for any activity in this area between the fourth and the ninth centuries and no physical evidence from St Peter's itself. On a parallel with Lincoln we might expect a British cemetery, for example, if there had been a Christian community in London at this time.

On the Continent many of the religious centres grew up around the graves of saints and martyrs who had been buried in the extra-mural cemeteries which ringed the Roman cities. At Xanten in Germany the medieval town surrounds the cemetery while the Roman town was abandoned. In Britain a similar situation can be seen at St Albans. St Alban was martyred in the second century and his shrine was visited by St Germanus of Auxerre in 429 (Borius 1965), which may imply that the Christian community there had already been worshipping at his grave for over two centuries. Gildas, writing in the north in the sixth century, was the first to specify that the shrine was at Verulamium and indicates that the cult was still active at that time, although the northern British could not then travel to the shrine. In the late eighth century a monastery dedicated to St Alban was founded by Offa. The community must therefore have survived the antagonism towards the British church typified by Bede in the early eighth century. Further west this survival may be quite common, or so place-name evidence suggests, but in the south-east of England it is, so far as we know, unique. As at Xanten, the church at St Albans eventually became the focus for the medieval town, leaving Verulamium decaying in the valley. Excavations by Martin Biddle have confirmed that a late Roman (Christian?) cemetery lay on the hill to the south of the abbey. They have also shown that a large number of coins were lost in this graveyard and it is likely that this is evidence that trade took place under the protection of St Alban. This gives a hint of the importance that a religious centre could have within the Roman period. Later, when Verulamium itself had fallen into ruin, the church of St Alban would naturally have become a meeting place for the Christians of the surrounding district.

In London, neither Smithfield nor Bishopsgate became a Christian focus, so far as we know, and both had reverted to agriculture by the end of the Saxon period. Where extra-mural settlement is known, along the Strand, there is no evidence that there was ever a large late Roman cemetery although, like most approach roads to Roman cities, there were burials along its length (RCHM 1928). The church of St Martin-in-the-Fields has several claims to be an early church, certainly earlier than the first surviving documentary reference which dates to the beginning of the thirteenth century. First, there is the fact that it was the centre of a late thirteenth-century treasure hunt:

Also in this yere men of London wenten and sercheden the chirche of Seynt Martyns in the feld for tresoure of gold, thorough the wordes of a gardyn', whiche seyde how there was a gold hord; but they found mought: wherefore the dene of Poules of London, be comaundement of the erchebyshop of Caunterbury, denounced them alle accursed openly at the Cross of Poules that sergeden as above seyd (London 1827, 39).

This, combined with the discovery of a late sixth or early seventh-century burial under the portico of the church in the early eighteenth century, suggests that there may have been a rich Anglo-Saxon cemetery in the area. Whether this cemetery was Christian or not is less easy to tell. The presence of Christian symbolism on many seventh-century grave goods in Anglo-Saxon cemeteries suggests that the custom of burying the dead with their belongings survived the conversion of the Anglo-Saxons to Christianity. A parallel for burial with a glass bowl in a stone coffin, presumably a reused Roman coffin, can be found at Peterborough Cathedral (Harden 1956, 165 Type Xd2), in a context which must surely be associated with the major Anglo-Saxon monastery of *Medeshamstede*, the original name for Peterborough. The possibility that the St Martin's burial was pagan should not be forgotten. Amongst the finds described at the time of its discovery were a large number of cattle skulls. Excavations at Yeavering in Northumberland on a site identified as the palace of Edwin of Northumbria revealed a structure from which many cattle skulls were recovered and which on this evidence has been interpreted as a pagan temple. As the future Bishop of London, Mellitus, set out for England, Pope Gregory instructed him to found churches on the sites of pagan temples and St Martin's could therefore be an example of this process (Whitelock 1968, No. 151 Chxxx, 602).

The main church in London in the seventh century, however, was that of the Cathedral of St Paul. Bede describes the founding of the church in 604 and the conversion of the East Saxons. He also describes how the sons of the East Saxon King Saberht encouraged paganism on their father's death in 616, expelling the bishop. In Kent, the new King Eadbald could not re-established the East Saxon Church and no further mention is made of London or its bishop until the 660s, when Cedd became Bishop of the East Saxons. Bede states that the East Saxons had remained pagan until King Sigeberht was converted in 653. There is no documentary link between Cedd and London and it is possible that the western part of the East Saxon kingdom was still pagan at that time. The name used for Harrow in a charter of 767 suggests that it had been a pagan temple (the sanctuary of the Gumenings) but when it ceased to be used is unknown (Whitelock 1968, No. 73, 461). During the seventh century Christianity had varied success in the countryside. Burials such as those found underneath the kitchen of Northolt Manor belong to a transitional phase when in many parts of the country the original pagan cemetery was abandoned but replaced by another cemetery close by. Such burials might be accompanied by a long knife, known as the *seax* (Evison 1961, 226–30) and a few might have jewellery, but in general they were much less richly furnished than earlier burials. It has been suggested that these cemeteries were those of the first Saxons to be converted to Christianity (Meaney and Hawkes 1970, 45–55).

St Paul's Cathedral may therefore have had an insecure start in the early seventh century. It could have been abandoned until the 650s, although there is no reason to suppose that the church founded by Mellitus in 604 was not on the site later occupied by the cathedral. From the late seventh century onwards the documentary evidence for bishops styled 'of London' is continuous and if sites were to become available for excavation we should expect to find traces of a small community inside Ludgate from at least this date onwards. The history of the fabric of St Paul's in the Saxon period is very poorly known, however, although entries in the *Anglo-Saxon Chronicle* suggest that the church was razed by fire in 962 (Whitelock 1968, No.1, 206). A tradition preserved by St Paul's claims that the original endowment of the cathedral was twenty-four hides, while it has been suggested that the Middlesex hundred of Ossulstone, which surrounds London, might reflect the extent of land at one stage held by St Paul's.

If London held a large permanent population in the late seventh to mid-ninth centuries it is unlikely that their religious needs could have been met by the cathedral alone. Excavations in mid-Saxon Southampton have revealed a small church with graveyard, while the church of St Mary at the southern end of the town may have existed from the beginning of the settlement. There is no reason why similar churches should not have existed in the Strand settlement but there is also no reason why they should have survived the depopulation of the settlement in the ninth century. By the thirteenth century there were five churches serving the area once occupied by the mid-Saxon settlement. Of these, the case for St Martin-in-the-Fields as possibly having an early origin has been presented. St Andrew's Holborn is also likely to have had an early origin. It was on the edge of the Westminster estate and was used as a boundary in the charter of 959 when it was known as the old wooden church of St Andrew. Any church said to be old in the middle of the tenth century must surely have been built in the ninth century or earlier and it is extremely unlikely that a church would be founded anew in the Strand area at a time when the settlement itself had just lost the majority of its inhabitants. The possibility exists that St Andrew was actually the main church of the settlement, and its eccentric position is not dissimilar to that of St Mary in Southampton. However, the church of St Mary-le-Strand may also have a claim to be of mid-Saxon origin, although merely on the basis that it is situated in the heart of the mid-Saxon settlement, was dedicated to St Mary and in the post-conquest period its patronage was claimed by Worcester Cathedral, which had strong connections with London in the eighth and ninth centuries (Dyson 1978, 205 and note 34). The fact that until the middle of the twelfth century it was dedicated to the Holy Innocents makes this claim even weaker (Brooke and Keir 1975, 140).

The remaining Strand churches are probably of later tenth or eleventh-century date. St Clement Danes was so called in the medieval period and two stories arose to account for it. In the first, recorded by the monks of Chertsey, the church was the site of a battle between the Vikings and Alfred, who chased them to London after their sacking of Chertsey. In the second, the church was the resting place of the body of Harold I, which the *Anglo-Saxon Chronicle* records was exhumed from Westminster by his half-brother Harthacnut and thrown into the fen, presumably the marshy mouth of the Tyburn known as *bulunga fen* and situated within the mid-tenth century bounds of the Strand estate. Florence of Worcester recounts that Harthacnut gave orders for the body to be thrown into the Thames. A short while afterwards it was picked up by a certain fisherman and borne in haste to the Danes and buried by them with honour in the cemetery which they had in London (Whitelock 1968, No. 9, 291). In 1927, Sir Mortimer Wheeler identified this cemetery with St Clement Danes which, like that of St Bride in Fleet Street, served a mid-eleventh-century Danish suburb extending along Fleet Street towards Westminster. Excavations at St Bride's Fleet Street showed that ecclesiastical use of the site began before the Norman conquest, but the detailed interpretation of the results is difficult. The earliest church found had a polygonal apse in the centre of which was a deep pit whose fill contained a sherd of mid-eleventh-century or later pottery (Grimes 1968, 182−8). However, a cemetery was found in which some burials were earlier than the church apse. The final church in the area of the mid-Saxon settlement is that of St Dunstan. The dedication of this church must post-date the death of the saint in 988 and, unless rededicated, it is therefore likely to be a late tenth-century or later foundation.

The Strand settlement may well have been an exception to the general rule, which is that there were relatively few churches in the seventh to ninth centuries and that the religious needs of the population were catered for by communities of clerics based in cathedrals, monasteries or minsters (*see* Fig. 31). Later in the medieval period these three types of church developed into quite separate institutions − minsters being approximate to collegiate churches − but in the mid-Saxon period their differences seem to have been blurred. For example, some monasteries were occupied by clerics, or laymen, who had not taken vows of celibacy. Many monasteries were founded during the late seventh and eighth centuries, a

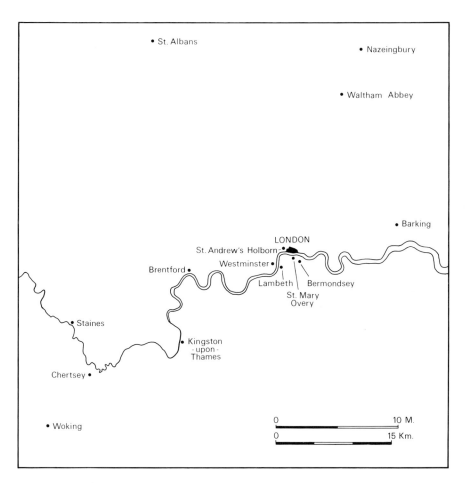

FIG. 31 Possible minster churches and monasteries in the London area in the seventh to ninth centuries. This is almost certainly a drastic under-estimate of the actual number of churches, although the majority of parish churches probably came into existence in the tenth or eleventh centuries.

time of great religious zeal. Later in the eighth century this zeal was concentrated in the conversion of the continental Germans, and London is noted as the point of departure of one such missionary, St Boniface, who sailed from London (*Lundenwic*) to Dorestad on the Rhine delta (Life of Boniface, Ch. 4). Some of these monasteries, such as Chertsey, St Alban's and Barking, were given quantities of land as endowments and grew to become wealthy and important medieval institutions. Others disappeared, a fate which was sometimes blamed on the Vikings. Chertsey and Barking both have traditions dating back to the medieval period that they were sacked by the Vikings and yet they survived or were refounded and re-endowed.

It is perhaps more likely that the monasteries which failed were the poorer ones which either failed during the eighth or ninth centuries or were not held in sufficient esteem in the tenth or eleventh centuries to attract a new founder. One such institution, a nunnery, was discovered by excavation at Nazeingbury, Essex (Huggins 1978). The excavation revealed a typical sequence of prehistoric to early Saxon rural settlement following which two timber buildings and a cemetery occupied the site. The identification of the site as a nunnery is based on the analysis of the skeletons in the cemetery by Glenys Putnam. Of those burials which could be sexed, eighty-six were females and thirty-two males. Only one of the females showed signs of having had children (illustrated by a notched pre-auricular sulcus) although the majority lived to old age. There was an abnormal divergence in build between the males and females and a few cases of 'well cared-for, highly pathological cases' (Huggins 1978, 63). These included a male, about thirty-five to forty-five years old, who had fatigue fractures of both feet. These are normally found in athletes, soldiers (from marching) and long-distance walkers. It is suggested that the person may have been a pilgrim. He was buried within the timber church. Some years after the excavation, a charter recording the foundation of the nunnery by King Suabred of Essex was discovered (Bascombe 1987, 85–96). Until then, the existence of the nunnery had been totally forgotten.

Two of the monasteries in the London area were founded by Eorcenwold, later Bishop of London, in the late seventh century. Chertsey was founded as a monastery for Eorcenwold himself while Barking was founded as a nunnery for his sister (Whitelock 1968, No. 151, 652). An early grant of land to Barking from Oethelraed, an East Saxon kinsman of King Sebbi, illustrates the way in which such communities could grow. Abbess Aethelburh received land at '*Ricingaham*, *Budinham*, Dagenham, *Angenlabeshaam* and the field in the wood that is called Widmund's field' all of which amounted to forty hides (Whitelock 1968, No. 60, 446–9). The exact location of this grant is not known but it must have formed a large block of territory around Barking. A similar grant was provided for Chertsey, in this case by Frithuwold, a sub-king of the province of Surrey. Frithuwold's grant included not only what is likely to have been a large block of rural property but also a small estate in or close to London, showing that from their foundation these mid-Saxon monasteries had an interest in marketing the produce from their estates (Whitelock 1968, No. 54).

Two abbeys were founded as offshoots of the great Mercian monastery of *Medeshamstede*, (Peterborough). They were at Woking and Bermondsey, the latter almost opposite the site of the Roman city of London. We know little of their foundation, their endowments or their fate. Neither survived into the tenth century. Excavations at Bermondsey on the site of an early Norman abbey, by David Beard for the Museum of London, have shown that there certainly was activity on the site in the mid-Saxon period. Two *sceattas* have been found, together with sherds of chaff-tempered and Ipswich-type ware pottery. Several gravel quarries, one containing an early to mid-Saxon loom weight, were excavated and a boundary ditch backfilled in the tenth or early eleventh century was discovered, but the excavated site itself seems to have been agricultural land, although probably very close to a settlement (Richardson 1987, 276). Other daughter foundations of Peterborough seem to have had a missionary function, for example Breedon-on-the-Hill in Leicestershire, but it is doubtful if this would have been the function of Bermondsey, from where it would have been possible to look across the river to St Paul's. Most likely they were founded to consolidate Mercian power in Surrey. Soon after 704, following the Synod of Brentford, Surrey was detached from the diocese of London and given to Winchester (Yorke 1985, 34).

Westminster Abbey, which by the end of the Saxon period was by far the richest and most influential monastery in the London area, has a very unclear history. The main reason for this is that during the late eleventh and early twelfth centuries vast quantities of deeds were fabricated there. These forgeries were sometimes based on original documents but do mean that almost every document preserved at Westminster in a late eleventh-century or later version is suspect. An account of the foundation written between 1076 and 1085 states that it was founded by an unnamed citizen of London during the life of Aethelberht of Kent, but there is no independent evidence for this. Richard Gem points out that this is the earliest foundation date which would sound plausible and by having an anonymous founder the story could not be contradicted by Bede (Gem 1986, 9). There are deeds recording the donation of land by Offa in the late eighth century and Offa too is said to have founded the abbey. Excavations under the Undercroft Museum in the abbey produced sherds of mid-Saxon pottery and an early ninth-century coin of Egbert of Wessex, showing that there was occupation on Thorney Island before the mid-tenth century, the date from which undeniable evidence for the existence of the abbey first survives.

Monastic life suffered badly during the Danish invasions of the ninth century and in the early tenth century there seems to have been little desire to revive it. However, the foundation and endowment of monasteries certainly underwent a rapid growth during the second half of the tenth century and one of the architects of this monastic revival was St Dunstan, briefly Bishop of London between 959 and 961. Dunstan reformed Westminster and was instrumental in providing a large endowment. Lists of the estates belonging to the mid-tenth century and later abbey show that it had acquired a considerable tract of land in north and west Middlesex. Bounds of some of the Westminster estates survive and provide an important source of information about Middlesex in the tenth century and before. The most interesting acquisition as far as this book is concerned was undoubtedly that of the estate which included the site of the mid-

Saxon *wic* and the lands which went with it. It is unlikely that this grant actually restored to Westminster rights over the *wic* which it had previously held — rights to toll, for example, were always granted by the king directly — but that is in effect what the preamble of the charter alleges (Gem 1986, 9–10).

We have no knowledge of the architecture or layout of Westminster in the tenth century, but to judge by its endowments it could have been substantial. Certainly it was sufficiently important to be the burial place of Harold I. In the reign of Edward the Confessor, however, the abbey was refounded on a massive scale in a development designed to create a royal palace complex incorporating a huge hall and a completely rebuilt church. The undercroft excavations mentioned above revealed a wide ditch, backfilled in *c.* 1050 or later, which may well have been the boundary ditch of the tenth-century abbey. Amongst the material thrown into it was a mass of potash-rich window glass, presumably derived from the tenth-century church. This is the earliest documented use of such glass (the standard type used in the medieval period) in the London area. A re-placement ditch produced a single decorated glazed floor tile, sparse evidence for the internal fittings of the church of the Confessor's abbey.

While it is quite clear that the major churches of the London area before the late ninth century were the monasteries described above, together with St Paul's, there is a further class of churches which should be of pre-Viking age, the old minsters. The term 'old minster' is first found in the Second Code of King Edgar, dated between 960 and 962, where three classes of church are referred to. At the bottom of the list came field churches, which had no burial rights, then churches on the bookland of thegns, with their own graveyards, and finally the old minsters. In the middle of the tenth century, therefore, churches within an estate — which later became parish churches — were probably a novel, numerous but by no means universal phenomenon. Originally, the diocese would have been organised through priests based in a series of churches, the old minsters, administered by the bishop. Gradually a situation came about whereby almost every estate, or group of estates under one landowner, had its own church, which later became the parish church. The old minster churches themselves shrank in importance as the tithes and congregations which once came to them were diverted to the newer churches. It has been found that the organisation of the church in this respect seems to mirror secular administration.

An old minster church is likely to be found at a site which was also a *villa regia* or king's *tun* and which might also be the site of a market or public (later 'hundredal') meeting place. Convincing cases of this arrangement have been documented by Jeremy Haslam in Wiltshire, where a number of small medieval towns can be seen to have their origins in such a royal-ecclesiastic centre. In modern Essex several places preserve the element '-minster' in their name, but in Surrey and Middlesex convincing evidence for such centres is sparse. Staines, however, is a documented minster site and also had a reeve, showing that it was a king's tun (Jones 1982, 191–3). Brentford was the meeting-place for the Church Synod in 781 and is almost certain therefore to have had a church. Kingston-upon-Thames is also likely to have had a minster church, especially as it was the site chosen for the consecration of Athelstan in 925 and Eadred in 948 (Whitelock 1968, No. 1, 199 and 203). St Mary's Lambeth is also a documented minster church, and is recorded in the Domesday Book as holding land in Gloucestershire. The hall at Lambeth is known from 1042 when Harthacnut collapsed there while standing at his drink. St Mary Overy, Southwark, was a priory founded in 1108 but it is thought to be on the site of an earlier church. Most ninth-century *burhs* were able to utilise earlier churches or were planned as forts rather than towns. It is most unlikely that Southwark would have been without a church in the late ninth century while there is no reason to suppose that Southwark would have made a suitable site for a mid-Saxon old minster. There is no evidence for mid-Saxon settlement in the numerous excavations carried out on the site of the Roman and medieval settlement. We may therefore have in St Mary Overy an unusual example of a late ninth or early tenth-century foundation, as at St Oswald's Priory in Gloucester (Heighway 1978). Recent excavation has tentatively suggested that there was a church at Waltham Abbey predating the foundation in *c.* 1030 by a Danish nobleman, Tovi, of a church to house a relic of the Holy Cross (Richardson 1987, 278). This church was itself rebuilt by Earl Harold in *c.* 1057/8 in a cruciform plan.

Given the link between minster churches and administrative centres, it is likely that there would have been a minster church within each hundred. Within Gore there are three likely candidates: Harrow, Hendon and Kingsbury. The latter is the most central to the hundred. The present church contains fragments of reused Roman tile but has no early features. Nevertheless, the name Kingsbury, together with the proximity of the hundredal meeting place at Gore, suggest that there may once have been a minster there. On the same criteria Isleworth may have been a minster while the hundred of Edmonton appears sometimes as the Half Hundred of Mimms, which is therefore likely to be the original centre.

The impression given by the evidence marshalled above is that before the Viking period almost all the major churches in the London area – Chertsey, Westminster, Bermondsey and Barking – were close to the Thames. They would therefore have been exceptionally vulnerable to Viking attack. Only those within the walls of the city would have had adequate protection. But it is unclear how many churches there were in the walled city at that time. St Paul's and St Peter Cornhill have been discussed above and the balance of probability is that St Peter is a late

Saxon foundation. Few other churches have any positive claims to be earlier than *c*. 1020, let alone the late ninth century. The first of these is All Hallows Barking, also known as All Hallows by the Tower. The evidence for an early origin for this church was revealed when the church was bombed during the Blitz. Fragments of carved cross-shaft and a grave-marker were found but these date to the middle of the eleventh century (*see* Fig. 32). A blocked doorway, however, could be much earlier (*see* Fig. 33). It incorporates Roman tile and was initially published as a seventh-century structure, because of parallels with Brixworth (now thought to be slightly later, perhaps eighth or ninth century), which is also built using tile. The fact that the tiles were not used radially as a true vault also suggests an early date. Furthermore, Harold Taylor has identified two further pieces of walling which appear to be of the same build as the doorway (Taylor and Taylor 1965, 339). One incorporated into the north aisle wall gives the width of the church, while the other forms a southern projection immediately east of the doorway. This projection could be from a porch, part of a transept, or from a side chapel (known in the Saxon period as a *porticus*). This part of the city seems to have been peripheral until the construction of the White Tower provided a focus in the late eleventh century. The alternative name for the church arises because it was at one time owned by Barking Abbey. It is possible that the

FIG. 32   Four views of a square-sectioned cross-shaft from All Hallows Barking. (Museum of London)

FIG. 33   The Saxon doorway at All Hallows Barking. (Museum of London)

nuns of Barking had a refuge within the Roman walls and built a church within it. It is, however, just as likely that the church at All Hallows was built in the tenth or eleventh century. The sculptural fragments certainly show that there was a wealthy community in the area by the middle of the eleventh century.

Another church which has been claimed as mid-Saxon is that of St Alban, Wood Street (Grimes 1968, 203–9). Excavations on the site after the war showed that the original building was a small two-cell structure (*see* Fig. 34). In size and dimensions this looks no different from many proven eleventh-century buildings and there is apparently no evidence from the excavation to confirm an early date. However, the church was identified by Thomas Walsingham, a medieval chronicler of St Alban's, as being the chapel of Offa's palace. In most cases such an unsubstantiated claim at such a late date would be dismissed, but two further pieces of circumstantial evidence give the claim more validity. First, there are a number of reasons for believing that a royal palace did lie to the north of St Paul's (*see* pages 54–6). Second, the church lies almost at the centre of the Cripplegate fort which could have survived into the Saxon period as a separately defended area within the city walls. Even so, the balance of probability is certainly heavily against it being anything other than a typical eleventh-century church.

St Mary Magdalen Milk Street was called a minster in a twelfth-century document and was in a central position within the late Saxon town, slightly set back from Cheapside. Little else is known of its history and the term 'minster' was sometimes given at that date as a 'courtesy title'. A tenth-century date could be claimed for St Benet Fink, since a grave-cover from the site of this church could stylistically be of late tenth-century date (*see* Fig.35). That such evidence is considered 'early' is an indication of the very late date at which the majority of the churches within the walls of London were probably founded.

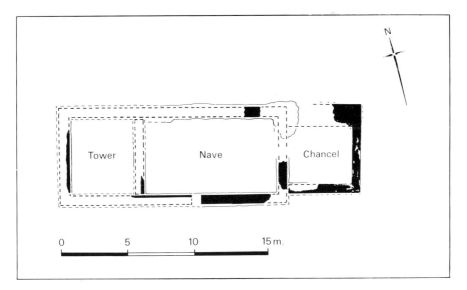

FIG. 34   Plan of the earliest stone church of St Alban, Wood Street as revealed by excavation (after Grimes). For the location of this church, at a street corner and entered from the street, see Fig. 29. Although two of the early walls are butt-jointed (that dividing the western tower from the nave and the south wall of the chancel) it is more likely that this church was conceived as a whole. The abnormal thickness of the north wall of the chancel is unexplained.

FIG. 35   A grave-cover of late tenth or eleventh-century date from St Benet Fink. (Drawn by Sue Mitford)

Notwithstanding the evidence from archaeology, dedications and historical records, it is very likely that ninth-century estates such as those at Queenhithe would have had churches or chapels within them for the use of the inhabitants, providing, that is, that they were ever occupied as coherent estates. When such an estate was subdivided into tenements the site of an earlier church or chapel should have been retained to serve the new tenants. However, even within the blocks of land divided by the Alfredian street-grid in the western part of the city, the churches are located on street frontages and particularly at the junctions of major streets. This suggests that they were sited for the convenience of a congregation living in approximately the same area as that defined by the later parish boundaries, which cut across the blocks, rather than to serve communities living within them.

By the twelfth century the pattern of parishes within the walls of London was already virtually complete and there are few churches which are not likely to have been in existence by the middle of the eleventh century, before the Norman conquest. This pattern has been established in many cities, not just London, and is the result of changing attitudes towards the foundation of churches − patrons, who in the eleventh century might have founded their own church, tended in later centuries to endow a chapel within an existing church. Furthermore, a point came when the city could not support any more churches. Churches were still being founded in the mid-eleventh century, as is shown by their dedications, for example of St Alphege, St Mildred, St Olave and St Nicholas. This is confirmed in some cases by archaeology, for example at St Nicholas Shambles, also known as St Nicholas Aldred, which appears to have been built on a plot once occupied by domestic buildings whose pits contain pottery of dates up to and including the middle of the eleventh century (*see* Fig. 36). St Nicholas Acon is similarly dated later than *c.* 1040 by pottery found in pits underneath its walls (Marsden 1967, 219–220) (*see* Fig. 37). In both cases the name of the founder was used to distinguish the church. In the first case the founder was Aldred, quite likely the same Aldred who gave his name to Aldersgate, while in the second case the founder had a Scandinavian name, Haakon.

One church with a late dedication, St Olave in the Jewry, has recently been excavated. The church may originally have had two parts, although the east end was destroyed in the nineteenth century and a western annexe, probably a tower, was constructed soon after the nave (Shepherd

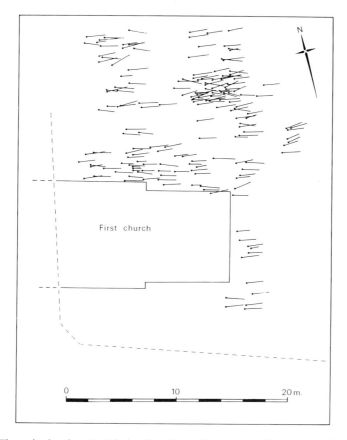

Fig. 36 The early church at St Nicholas Shambles and its cemetery. The church and its cemetery seem to occupy the sites of four earlier tenements and was probably founded in the middle of the eleventh century. Pits and a building ranging in date from the tenth to the middle of the eleventh century were found underlying burials. (Museum of London)

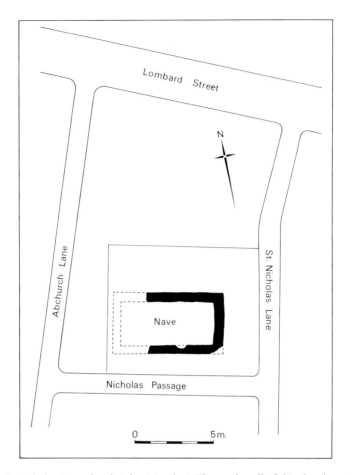

FIG. 37   St Nicholas Acon church (after Marsden). The north wall of this church overlay a pit backfilled in the middle of the eleventh century and other pits and refuse of this date lay within the area later occupied by the church. The boundary of the church and churchyard in the seventeenth century suggests that three earlier tenements were combined to form the church in the middle of the eleventh century. Nicholas Passage may have originated as an access to the south door of the church.

1987, 23–5). No dating evidence was found, apart from the reuse of Roman tile in the quoins, but the dedication is unlikely to have been given until after the death of King Cnut, who was responsible for the death of Olave. In one case a charter dated between 1052 and 1070 survives recording the intention of a citizen, called Brihtmaer of Gracechurch, to build a church, All Hallows Lombard Street, and grant it to Canterbury. In return, the founder became the first priest of the church and could live on the tithes given by his parish. Brihtmaer's church was excavated in 1939 and was shown to be aligned not east-west, nor on the Roman forum alignment (even though the church was sited over the south range of the forum) but perpendicular to Gracechurch Street (Oswald 1940,

51p). In all probability its position was governed by the dimensions of a domestic tenement running back from the street.

To judge by their location the majority of the churches within the walls started life in a similar way. They were founded on what had been a domestic tenement and therefore had to adapt to the constraints of space. Graveyards too seem to have served first as occupation sites. At Holy Trinity Priory, situated just inside Aldgate, a church is known to have existed prior to the construction of the priory in 1108. The precise location of the pre-priory church is not known but a section of the graveyard has been found (Riviere 1985/6, 37). Two quite distinct areas were recognised, separated by a fence (*see* Fig. 38). In one, burials had taken place for some time, leading to the superimposing of graves, while the other had been a domestic back yard, with pits and a well, until the mid to late eleventh century when it became an extension to the graveyard. This complex sequence of burials apparently built up in a very short time, since the church was recorded as being founded by Syredus, a canon of St Paul's who was still alive in 1066 (since he is recorded as holding land under King Edward in the Domesday Book).

From this combination of archaeological, documentary and dedicatory evidence it seems that there was a major period of church foundation in London in the reign of Edward the Confessor, although there were un-doubtedly earlier churches, a few of which may have been founded soon after the reoccupation of the city. Settlement was expanding in the late eleventh century around the tenth and early eleventh-century nucleus. Outside the walls were churches whose dedications are to saints whose cults were in the ascendant during the late eleventh or early twelfth

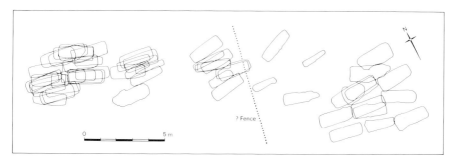

FIG. 38 Plan of part of a cemetery found under the church of Holy Trinity Priory, founded in the early twelfth century on the site of a church which was itself founded in the middle of the eleventh century by a canon of St Paul's, Syredus. The contrast in density of burials between the eastern and western halves of the excavated area suggests that the eastern half was acquired when the western half began to fill up. This hypothesis is supported by the fact that pits and a well ranging in date up to the middle of the eleventh century underlay the graves on the eastern half. Whether the whole cemetery is that of Syredus's church or whether the western half of the cemetery is earlier, starting in the later ninth or tenth centuries, and the eastern half belonged to Siward's church, remains to be discovered.

centuries – Holy Sepulchre outside Newgate, St Botolph outside Aldgate, Aldersgate and Bishopsgate, and St Giles outside Cripplegate. To the south, the demolition of the wall and the reclamation of the foreshore opened up a strip which was served by a series of churches which either definitely or probably came into existence at this time. St Botolph Billingsgate, for example, was constructed on new ground, as perhaps was St Magnus immediately to its west. At the western end of this waterfront churches such as St Benet and St Peter were constructed on old ground, north of the riverside wall, but the streets which lead north from the waterfront past these churches seems to have come into existence in the late eleventh century suggesting that there too the waterside churches are relatively late.

The outline development of the church in the London area is clearer now than it was a few years ago. The position of Westminster is now seen to have been immediately west of the mid-Saxon settlement and the origin of many city churches is now revealed by excavation. However, we still know very little indeed about late Roman Christianity and it must surely be only a matter of time before a Roman church is found in London. Much would be revealed if excavations could take place on the site of old St Paul's. Although it is possible that little remains of the Saxon church and its associated buildings, excavations in other cathedral precincts have shown that despite the generations buried in the graveyards and the disturbance caused by successive building programmes there is usually considerable information to be gained.

One of the most interesting areas which could be examined with the help of archaeology is that of the rural peasantry. We have seen how, in the tenth century, parish churches were still a novelty and how the archaeological evidence suggests that in London they were still scarce. We cannot tell where people went to hear the gospel or celebrate festivals, but we can tell where they were buried by discovering and excavating their cemeteries. The late pagan or early Christian burials at Northolt (Middlesex) and similar sites contain few datable artefacts and the end of the use of such a cemetery can only really be determined by repeated use of carbon dating. Once the age of these cemeteries has been established it will be clear whether they were superseded immediately by parish churches, whether minster churches were used for a while as regional graveyards, or whether parish churches were preceded by graveyards. Excavations at Aylesbury in Buckinghamshire have shown that the minster church there was surrounded by a vast cemetery, covering about a quarter of the area later occupied by the medieval town. But excavations at Little Ilford, Essex, have shown that the late eleventh-century timber church was later than at least one burial (Redknap 1985, 33).

Having found mid-Saxon London, the next task is to find some mid-Saxon Londoners.

7 Defence

To anyone sailing up the Thames in the later fourth century London must have been an impressive sight. Further down river there would have been signal stations. These were defended towers built in the later third century, from which a watch was kept for hostile craft. One such tower has been found, at Shadwell (Johnson 1975, 278–80). If anything was spotted, a beacon would have been lit and the information sent back to London where guards manning the city walls would have taken action, closing the gates and mustering the defence force. Supplies of grain and livestock would also have needed to be present if the town was to withstand a lengthy attack.

There were five or six landward gates in the city wall, although little is known of their later Roman form. From the east the first is Aldgate. Next, Bishopsgate may have been rebuilt in a slightly different position, since the stretches of Roman road leading towards it indicate an opening to the west of the medieval gate. That at Aldersgate was approximately on the site of the medieval gate and was revealed by excavation in the 1920s. On the west side of the city, Newgate is undoubtedly a Roman gate, through which the road later to become known as Oxford Street and High Holborn entered the city. There may have been a gate on the site of Ludgate. Smaller gates existed on the site of the west and north gates of the Cripplegate fort, while there has recently been a suggestion that there may have been a gate somewhere in the stretch of wall to the south of Tower Hill (Haslam 1988). The stretch of wall which survives there, to the north of the Tower of London, gives a good impression of the scale of the defences. It would have stood to a height of about five metres and would originally have had an earthen rampart piled against its inner face. A wall walk ran along the top of the wall and guards would have been protected by battlements, although these were replaced by medieval work along the whole circuit.

Along the eastern and north-eastern side of the wall were a series of semi-circular bastions. These were built some time in the middle of the fourth century and reuse monumental architecture, such as tombstones, altars and large fragments of ashlar in their foundations. The construction of the bastions was accompanied by the replacement of the original narrow V-shaped ditch by a much wider, U-shaped ditch dug further from the wall to accommodate the bastions. The bastions were filled with earth, supposedly to support large catapults, or similar artillery, which were used to shoot stones and other missiles. The wide ditch would have kept any attackers far enough away to be within range of the artillery. There is no archaeological evidence that bastions were added to the riverside wall, although Fitzstephen stated that they did exist and it has been postulated that the Wakefield, Lanthorn and Bell Towers in the Tower of London are sitting on Roman foundations (Parnell 1981, 73).

We know little about the manning of the walls. It is assumed that the presence of artillery would require professional soldiers, but military equipment in the late Roman army seems to have been less diagnostic than in the early Empire, when it is possible to recognise the presence of the army through numerous dress fittings and armour fragments. The most diagnostic features of late Roman military equipment are the buckles and fittings from a wide belt from which hung the soldier's equipment. Characteristics of the buckle are the use of zoomorphic terminals and the buckle plate is often decorated with chip-carved geometric designs. Unfortunately, these characteristics are typical of developments in late Roman art and it is not possible to positively identify all military buckles. However, there is a general consensus that a buckle found at Smithfield in the nineteenth century and now in the British Museum (*see* Fig. 30) is from the burial of a late fourth or early fifth-century soldier (Hawkes and Dunning 1961, 62, Type IVA). Recent excavations have failed to add to the corpus of late Roman military equipment from London, but this corresponds to the paucity of late fourth-century material from the city as a whole.

A stretch of the city wall along the riverside, found at the site known as Baynard's Castle at the south-west corner of the city, may well have been rebuilt at the same time as the bastions were added. It contained reused stones from a monumental arch as well as two altars (*see* Fig. 39). Initially it was thought that the whole of the riverside wall dated to the fourth century because of radiocarbon dating of its oak piles, but in 1983 it was realised that this was incorrect, since the timber could then be dated more precisely by dendrochronology to the mid to late third century. It is therefore about half a century later than the dated parts of the landward wall (Sheldon and Tyers 1983, 359–61). However, the piles were under an earlier stretch of wall, perhaps part of the original circuit in this area of the city, while the reused stones were in a stretch of wall erected without piles much of which, significantly, had eventually tumbled onto the Thames' foreshore.

In one further area along the riverside the city wall was repaired in the late Roman period but there are several reasons for believing that this was a different, and much later, piece of work. The stretch of wall in question was in the south-east corner of the city and lies almost immediately under the Edwardian defences of the Tower of London. Here, the original third-

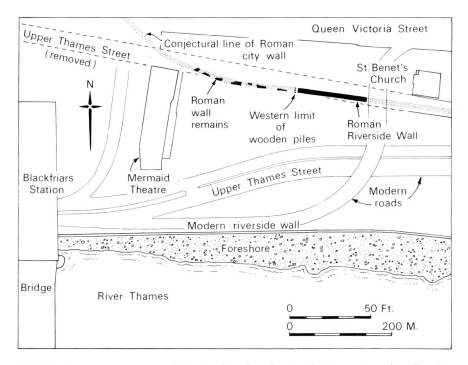

FIG. 39 The south-west corner of the city of London, showing the Roman riverside wall and its relationship with Upper Thames Street and the modern river frontage.

century wall survives as footings but a new wall was constructed behind it. The space between and behind the walls was filled with refuse. Coins found amongst the refuse date it to the last two decades of the fourth century or later. The most striking aspect of this wall, however, is that in contrast to the bastions and the Baynard's Castle wall it was built in fresh stone, and to a high standard (*see* Fig. 40). This wall is the latest dated Roman defensive wall unearthed in Britain and it is extremely likely that it was built by the Roman general Stilicho, who came to Britain in the 390s to restore the defences of the province (Hill 1980, 70).

It has been suggested that the Tower wall was not a refurbishment of the whole circuit but part of a smaller fort, underlying and perhaps determining the position of the White Tower (Parnell 1981, 73). The evidence for such a fort may survive within the medieval wall circuit and if one did exist it would be of considerable importance for the understanding of the later defensive potential of the city. Another possibility is that the new wall was part of a platform built to take artillery.

The fifth-century British would undoubtedly have inherited a fortification in good order but would have needed a substantial garrison to hold it. The possible repositioning of Bishopsgate and the tradition recorded by Stow that Newgate was so named because it had been built by Henry I or

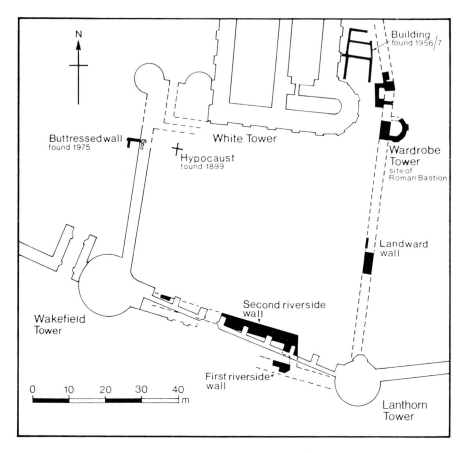

N

Buttressed wall
found 1975

White Tower

Hypocaust
found 1899

Building
found 1956/7

Wardrobe
Tower
site of
Roman Bastion

Landward
wall

Second riverside
wall

Wakefield
Tower

0   10   20   30   40
                         m

First riverside
wall

Lanthorn
Tower

FIG. 40   The location of the late Roman wall at the Tower of London. (G. Parnell, English Heritage)

Stephen hint that perhaps some of the gates were blocked to make the circuit easier to defend (Kingsford 1971, 35). This certainly happened to the south gate of Winchester in the late Roman period or later (Biddle 1975, 117–8).

The tradition recorded in the *Anglo-Saxon Chronicle* that the Britons had fled to London after the Battle of *Crecganford* in 457 may reflect the use of London as either a retreat or a stronghold. Other references to the British use of Roman walls for defence in the fifth century and later are to be found in the *Chronicle*. The inhabitants of Pevensey were slain by the Saxons in 491 and the entry for 577 implies that Gloucester, Bath and Cirencester were flourishing, each under its own king. Pevensey was a fortress rather than a town and was much smaller than London. It may prove to have harboured a British settlement, although there is no archaeological evidence for it yet. The remaining three cities have each been the subject of intense archaeological investigation but there is so far no evidence for any use of the defences in the fifth century. The type of fortification which the British would have been capable of constructing can be shown by excavations at South Cadbury in Somerset. There, the hilltop was refortified with a drystone wall (Alcock 1972, 175−7). Further west the small ring-work of Dinas Powys was constructed in the fifth or sixth century (Alcock 1963, 26−30). Its defences consisted of earth ramparts. The length of circuit of the walls of London is much larger than any of the other fortifications known to have been used by the British. It is therefore likely, if there is any historical fact behind the *Chronicle* entry, that the use of London's city walls was a passive act taking the existing defences and manning them for the duration of a crisis only.

The existence by the end of the seventh century of a large urban settlement along the Strand raises the question of what use, if any, was made of the city defences. A small area within the walls was occupied by the cathedral, but it seems that the early cathedral occupied a separate space within the walls, termed *Paulesbyri* in a charter dating between 704 and 709 (Gelling 1979, No. 193, 96). Other mid-Saxon religious establishments were based within Roman walls, but if the Roman walls proved too big the church normally took a section of the walled area and if necessary used Roman walls for two sides of their precinct and built their own boundary along the other two sides. In the case of London, the whole of the walled area of the city may have been used in some way by the cathedral, perhaps for orchards, gardens or fields. The city walls would then have acted as the precinct of the cathedral complex. Alternatively, the cathedral and its ancillary buildings may have been restricted to *Paulesbyri* and some other use may have been made of the walls.

One of the perplexing features of the mid-Saxon *wics* is that even when there was a suitable defended enclosure nearby they were sited on virgin ground instead. In the ninth century, when towns such as London, York and Southampton are known to have been attacked by the Vikings, this strategy strikes the modern observer as perverse. York and London, however, share one archaeological feature which may go some way towards explaining the role of the Roman walls. In both cases coins and metalwork of mid-Saxon date have been found within the walls, although occupation deposits have not. In York coin hoards of Anglian date have been found on the site of the Roman *colonia*, south of the River Ouse, while there is a scatter of metalwork on the site of the fortress, to the north of the Ouse and closer to the presumed site of the Anglian *wic* at Fishergate. It stretches credulity a little to suggest that the Anglians of York, upon being attacked by raiders sailing up the Ouse, would cross the river by boat, or bridge, and so lay themselves open to increased danger. Mid-Saxon towns such as Ipswich had no Roman walls for their inhabitants to run to, although at Ipswich too there is a site close to the town where numerous *sceattas* have been found. Excavations at this site, Barham, an

Iron Age hillfort, revealed little sign of mid-Saxon occupation (Youngs *et al* 1984, 240).

Sceattas are often found in or close to hillforts and it may be that the mid-Saxon finds from within the walls of London are comparable. These finds could be the result of the use of hillforts and Roman walled enclosures as refuges, but another possibility is that they were the sites of markets or fairs. Excavations at hillforts such as Danebury in Hampshire or Maiden Castle in Dorset have shown that these places were used for social and religious gatherings from the Neolithic period onwards and a number of medieval fairs were held on the site of hillforts. In short, we have no real idea what the walls of Roman London were used for in the mid-Saxon period. There is nothing yet to compare with the Anglian tower at York which shows that the defences of the fortress at York were being repaired at some stage between the end of the Roman occupation and the establishment of the Anglo-Scandinavian town. It is fairly certain, however, that the Strand settlement itself was not defended, since none of its sister settlements had defences. A ditch found on the Maiden Lane site may be of mid-Saxon date, although it cut through all other mid-Saxon features on the site, but its profile – vertical sides and flat bottom (*see* Fig. 41) – shows that it was only open for a short time and would have been totally unsuitable for defence (Cowie 1987, 32).

In 871 London must have passed into the temporary control of the Vikings, who took winter quarters there. The following year the host moved north, wintering at Torksey. Little is known of the defences used by the Viking army. No ninth-century defences are known in the Viking homeland, although they were capable in the eighth century of constructing the Danevirke, a dyke cutting off the Danish peninsula at its narrowest point. Their town of Haithabu/Hedeby, the predecessor of Sleswig, had no defences until the tenth century.

Contemporary records show that both the English and the Vikings used Roman fortifications for defence in emergencies. In 860 the Vikings had stormed Winchester, which was successfully defended by the Ealdormen of Hampshire and Berkshire and their levies (ASC Sa. 860; Whitelock 1968 No. 1, 175). It is possible that Winchester at that time contained the seventh-century cathedral and little else, but the fact that the West Saxons were able to muster the levies of two shires and reach Winchester before the Viking host had been able to march from the coast to the walls of Winchester, a distance of only twenty-one kilometres, shows at least that the defences of their kingdom were well organised. In 867 the Vikings had gone to York and while they were inside the city it was stormed by the Northumbrian levies. The Northumbrians entered the city but lost the battle, their two kings being killed and the remnant making peace with the Vikings. Current thinking suggests that the abandonment of the *wic* site at Fishergate and the occupation of the Roman fortifications at York

FIG. 41 A ditch or trench at the Maiden Lane, dated to the early ninth century or later and cutting through late eighth to ninth-century pits. Looking east. (Department of Greater London Archaeology, Museum of London)

dates from this period (Hall 1988, 129–30). The records therefore show that both the English and the Vikings were adept at siege warfare by the middle of the ninth century.

Events in the London area between 874 and 886 are difficult to establish. In 877 the Vikings had divided up Mercia, leaving their puppet king, Ceolwulf II, in control of the western half of the kingdom. London was presumably in Ceolwulf's portion but two years later, in 879, a band of Vikings took up quarters at Fulham. Their camp is traditionally said to have been on the site of the bishop's palace, which sits within a rectangular bank and ditch beside the Thames (*see* Fig. 42). It is quite likely that in

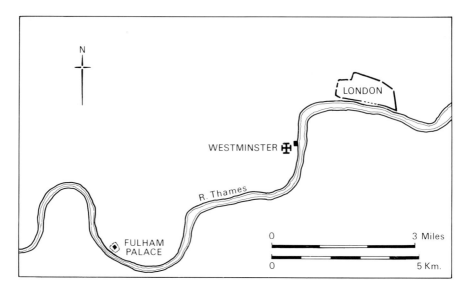

FIG. 42 The location of Fulham palace. The palace, probably a residence of the bishops of London from the time they acquired the estate in the eighth century, is traditionally said to be the winter camp of a Viking horde who over-wintered at Fulham in 871. Unexpectedly, the defences of the palace have been shown by excavation to date, in all probability, to the late Roman period.

the ninth century it would have been surrounded by water, or at least marsh. Excavations on the defences failed to find any trace of Viking activity but appear to show that the defences are of late Roman date (Arthur and Whitehouse 1978, 54–7). As in the city itself, it is probable that even after five hundred years these defences would have needed little work to be usable. The Fulham Vikings moved on to Ghent the following year, 880. A few years later Ceolwulf died and, according to Florence of Worcester, Alfred then 'in order to expel completely the army of the pagan Danes from his kingdom, recovered London with the surrounding areas by his activity, and acquired the part of the kingdom of the Mercians which Ceolwulf had held' (Whitelock 1968, 183). According to Alfred's biographer Asser, London was taken 'after the burning of cities and the massacre of people' (ASC sa. 886; Whitelock 1968, 183). These events are usually placed in 886 but the *Anglo-Saxon Chronicle* entry for 883 appears to have been misplaced and implies that the West Saxons fought against the Viking host who were within the walls of London:

> . . . and the same year Sigehelm and Athelstan took to Rome, and also to India to St Thomas and to St Bartholomew, the alms which king Alfred had vowed to send thither when they besieged the host in London; and, by the mercy of God, they were very successful in their prayers in accordance with those vows (Whitelock 1968, No. 1, 181; ASC sa. 883).

It is quite possible, given the confusing events of this period and the limited contemporary records, that the Vikings had retained London when dismembering Mercia in 877, in which case Alfred could have fought against them at any time up to 886. Ceolwulf's successor, Ethelred, is first recorded signing a charter dated 880 which is assumed to be a mistake for 887 and definitely granted land at Stoke Bishop to Berkeley Abbey in 883 (Sawyer 1986, Nos. 217 and 218). It is therefore worth bearing in mind that Alfred could have captured London as early as 880 or 883 but that there may have been a nine-year Viking occupation of London.

Well before the Viking incursions of the ninth century there are references within Anglo-Saxon charters to the duties of bridgework and *burhwork*. For example, a grant of land at Harrow was confirmed in 801 by Pilheard, *comes* of Cenwulf of Mercia. The land was to be free for ever from the rendering of all dues except 'the three public causes, that is, the construction of bridges and forts, and also, in the necessity of military service, only five men are to be sent' (Whitelock 1968, 461–2). It seems that the burden of constructing and maintaining these public works was apportioned estate by estate according to the value of the land. The meaning of *burhwork* in the Harrow charter is further elucidated by an earlier Mercian charter of 770, the first authentic charter to mention these public duties. The document states that land at Aston Fields, Worcestershire, was not to be free from the duty of providing 'the necessary defences of fortresses against enemies' (Whitelock 1968, 463).

From the late eighth century onwards we know that the term *burh* was being used to denote a fortress maintained by all the people. However, we are unclear as to the exact nature of an eighth-century *burh*. It might, for example, have been small enough to enclose an aristocratic residence such as a king's tun, or large enough to form a refuge for the whole population. The term *burh* is the ancestor of the modern word 'borough', which implies a legally established urban community. Originally, however, the word meant 'defensive enclosure' and is used in place-names to denote Iron Age hillforts and Roman camps as well as what might be contemporary Anglo-Saxon fortified places. By the end of the Anglo-Saxon period the term was being used to denote a manor or residence, as in Finsbury, named after an eleventh-century canon of St Paul's, or Bucklersbury, named after a thirteenth-century owner. Further confusion is added because the Anglo-Saxon term for hill or mound, *beorg*, came to be corrupted to *-bury* or *-borough*. The name *Lundenburh* or similar forms occurs in documents of the mid-ninth century or later (*see* Fig. 43) and by that date there is little else which could be meant by the name except that there was a fortification belonging to London, or that London itself was fortified.

By the end of the ninth century the West Saxons had adopted a policy of providing public *burhs* as places of refuge for the surrounding country-

Lundenwic

Lundenburh

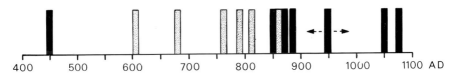

400   500   600   700   800   900   1000   1100 AD

FIG. 43 The names used for London in Anglo-Saxon documents. The '-wic' names cease at about the time of the movement of the settlement into the walled city. (Information supplied by John Clark, Museum of London)

side, and the timing of this innovation (and the precedence of the Mercians) is shown by the activities of the Viking army. An entry in the *Anglo-Saxon Chronicle* for 868 refers to the Vikings taking winter quarters in the *burh* of Nottingham, whereas in 876 the Vikings slipped past the West Saxons to enter Wareham, which Asser tells us was a nunnery with natural defences, except on the west where it joined the mainland. Wareham was certainly later a public *burh* and retains its Saxon earthen defences to this day. Excavations at Hereford have also suggested that the Mercians were providing *burhs* at an earlier date than the West Saxons, although the excavations provided no absolute dating evidence (Shoesmith 1982, 76–7, Stage One). This leaves open the possibility that London was provided with a public defence by the Mercians before 886. Indeed, it is difficult to suggest where else the peasants of Harrow could have been expected to do their *burhwork*. The core of that defence would undoubtedly have been the Roman walls but the city ditch might have been re-dug and a garrison provided.

A document known as the *Burghal Hidage* has some bearing on the status of London's defences in the late ninth or early tenth century. The original form of the document has been established by David Hill (1969). It consisted of a list of *burhs* with the number of hides which went with them. At the end of the list was a formula which enabled the user to calculate the length of wall which could be defended by a given area of land, assuming that each hide gave one man and that four men could defend a pole of the circuit (defined as sixteen and a half feet, or just over five metres). The *burhs* are listed in a clockwise direction around Wessex. Mercia is omitted, except for Oxford and Buckingham, and the document ends by stating that the *burhs* are West Saxon. Hill accepted Oxford as part of the original document but thought that Buckingham was an addition (Hill 1969, 88). This would date the original document to the period after 911, when eastern Mercia was annexed by Edward the Elder. London, in Hill's view, is excluded because it stood outside the system. Professor Davis of the University of Birmingham suggests that the *Burghal Hidage* dates to the reign of Alfred, at a time when London was still in Viking hands (Davis 1982). If so, it would date the fortification of Southwark to the 870s or 880s.

Whatever the date and precise meaning of the *Burghal Hidage*, it is quite conceivable that London was a public *burh* from the late ninth century (if not a century before) and, if so, that we can learn more of what might have been happening within the walls from a consideration of the Burghal Hidage *burhs*. There is doubt about the identity of some of the sites, including Southwark, since the name used could mean 'work of the southern people' (*i.e.* the men of Surrey), rather than 'the southern work' (*i.e.* in relation to London). However, there is enough agreement to see that not all the sites included were of equal size or status. Roman fortifications such a Portchester were present, as were simple promontory forts, defended by a single bank and ditch across a spur, the other sides being defended by a steep drop or by water. The most interesting sites are undoubtedly those like Cricklade or Wallingford which were defended solely by new Anglo-Saxon defences. These sites have a rectilinear plan and quite often went on to form the nucleus of a medieval town. Cricklade, however, hardly grew beyond a village until the 1970s when modern housing development started. It has received much attention from archae-ologists (Radford 1972; Haslam 1986, 99–103). Jeremy Haslam has shown that it must have been built to a metrical plan. A road was laid to form a square and on the outside of this road an earthen bank was constructed using the upcast from two narrow ditches. A narrow line of stones inside the intramural street is thought by the excavator to limit the area reserved to the king because of its strategic importance.

The existence of a similar zone on either side of the Roman city wall in London is shown both by documentary evidence (Jones 1956, 3–16), by archaeological evidence from the Old Bailey site, dug by Peter Marsden, and by the line of the city ditch and the roads which ran along its outer edge (for example Houndsditch). At the Old Bailey site the area immediately behind the city wall was heavily pitted in the late eleventh to mid-twelfth centuries but there was a zone without pits running parallel with the wall (*see* Fig. 44). Few pits earlier than the late eleventh century were found and this may be either because the area to the west of the cathedral was not developed until quite late or because occupation was not allowed to encroach upon the defences. The pit-free zone found in the excavation may mark the position of a rampart, later removed.

The only evidence for any activity close to the defences in the mid-Saxon period consists of sherds of chaff-tempered and Ipswich wares from a marsh deposit found where the riverside wall was crossed by the later Thames Street. These sherds may have been associated with an attempt to fill the marsh, represented by a deposit of rubble in the upper fill of the marsh (Millett 1980, 14) (*see* Fig. 12). It would, however, be stretching the evidence too far to see these stones as any sort of evidence for an intramural street. It has been suggested that Thames Street began life as a street running at the back of the standing riverside wall. At Peter's Hill, where an area was excavated immediately north of the wall,

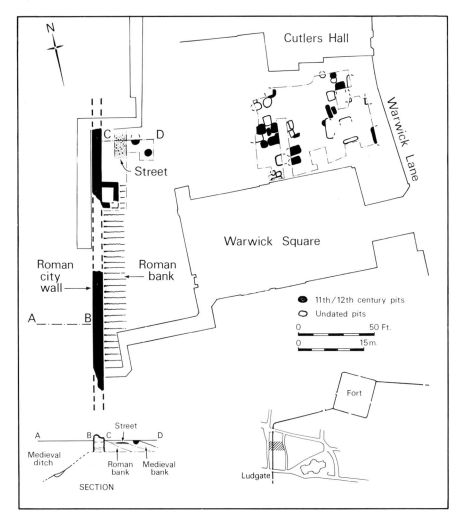

FIG. 44 The Central Criminal Court, Old Bailey, excavations (after Marsden). Unlike most areas of the city, few, if any, tenth to mid eleventh-century pits were found in the excavations. The area may therefore have deliberately been kept clear for defensive reasons.

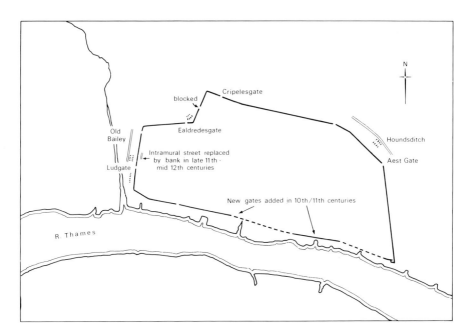

FIG. 45 The late Saxon defences of London. Excavated portions of the late Saxon or early Norman city ditch are shown, together with documented gates. The streets of Old Bailey and Houndsditch mark the outer lip of the city ditch and may be part of a once-continuous road running round the city.

the inner face of the city wall was found with Thames Street running right up to it. Pottery in the first make-up shows that the street was undoubtedly not constructed until the late eleventh or early twelfth centuries, as previously demonstrated by Charles Hill and Martin Millett further west (Hill 1980, 72), although they dated the construction rather too late because of the available knowledge of pottery chronology. No signs of any earlier street running parallel to the wall were seen in the Peter's Hill excavation and it is likely that there never was a late Saxon intramural street in this part of the circuit. There does, on the other hand, appear to have been a road running around the outer lip of the city ditch from an early date, since Old Bailey and Houndsditch appear to fossilise the eleventh or twelfth-century ditch line.

The archaeology of the ditch system surrounding the city walls is extremely difficult to disentangle since the ditches were originally dug in the late second or early third century, were then widened in the fourth century and finally recut in the twelfth and thirteenth centuries. After that time they were allowed to silt up or were backfilled, except where they were used as a watercourse, such as the Walbrook at Moorfields. Evidence for any Saxon refurbishment of the ditches has to be distinguished from earlier and later features (*see* Fig. 45). Excavations immediately outside the walls have taken place at several sites, among them Houndsditch

(Maloney and Harding 1979, 350−3), Cripplegate, directed by Professor Grimes, Aldersgate, excavated by Geoff Egan, and at the south end of Old Bailey (Rowsome 1984). The latter excavations showed that there had been several ditches in the area and that they had been dug progressively closer to the city wall. The filling of one of these ditches (Ditch Two) contained mid-eleventh-century or later pottery and may therefore be of late Saxon date. At Aldersgate only one city ditch, the outermost, was seen in the excavation. It contained a pattern-welded knife and a fragment of crucible, both of which should date to the eleventh century. At Cripplegate the area immediately outside the gate had been occupied in the eleventh century and the remains of these timber buildings were cut by a late medieval ditch/watercourse. Finally, at Houndsditch, a ditch was found which must have run just inside the line of the street. After it had been filled in it was covered with layers of gravel metalling and a new ditch was dug closer to the city wall. There was very little dating evidence from the first ditch except in its upper fill, which contained a leather shoe of probable twelfth-century date. These observations seem to show that the city ditch was re-dug during the late Saxon period, although none of the finds would preclude a conquest period or later digging. The Saxo-Norman city ditch seems to have been wide and flat-bottomed, very much like its late Roman predecessor. We do not know whether the space between its inner lip and the wall was a wide berm or whether there was another ditch, as at Cricklade. After this ditch was backfilled, or in at least one case had naturally silted up, it was re-dug closer to the city wall.

It has been claimed that the 'fish-bone' street plan seen in a number of the larger *burhs* is Alfredian in date, which may well be true, and devised for a strategic function, which is much less certain (Biddle and Hill 1971). At Winchester the side streets could have helped the garrison to rush to the walls and gates when the *burh* was under attack. However, it can be seen in London that there are two street grids which might be said to have a central spine with side streets, but in neither case do the streets end up at the walls (*see* page 124). Another feature of these planned *burhs*, such as Wareham and Cricklade, is that they have a church with a bell tower forming one side of one of the gates. Even after archaeological investigation it is not clear whether these churches are contemporary or later than the *burh* defences but the tower could have had the dual purpose of being a watchtower and a means of calling the faithful to prayer. In London, with its Roman gates, this may not have been so necessary and in many cases (*see* pages 75−6) it is likely that the churches just inside or outside the gates are of much later date. In one example however, St Martin Ludgate, there is a possibility that the church might actually either have been built into the gate-tower or sat just inside the wall (Rowsome 1984). The church of St Alphege was built into the north wall of the Cripplegate Fort, presumably some time after 1023 when the saint's body was translated from St Paul's to Canterbury (Westman 1987, 18). The tower of this church would have been ideally situated to keep a watch on Cripplegate, a short distance to the west.

Like the Roman defences, late Saxon London was provided with a warning system of lookouts and beacons. The one documented site was situated just to the south of Westminster and is recorded by a place-name, Tothill, which incorporates the Old English element *twt*, meaning a 'lookout'. At the latest, therefore, this lookout should be of early twelfth-century date and is first recorded in the late twelfth century. A hill, *hlaw*, which is probably Tothill, was used as a boundary in the mid-tenth-century bounds of Westminster's Strand estate. No natural hill would be expected on the gravel terrace at Westminster but of course an earlier mound could have been used by the Saxons. An observer on top of Tothill could have seen anyone trying to cross the river at the Westminster ferry, anyone sailing down river and anyone using the old Roman road, Fleet Street and the Strand. No other lookouts are documented or recorded by place-names in the London area but there are mounds recorded in the London area which may well have been part of this system. Whitechapel Mount, for example, lay to the south of Mile End road just to the east of the city. However, it is the findspot of a necklace now in the collection of the Society of Antiquaries which is thought to be of early Anglo-Saxon date. Perhaps the mount was an Anglo-Saxon or earlier barrow, but since it no longer exists there is little chance that we will ever know its function.

The way in which the defences of London were to be manned is a matter of considerable speculation. Which areas had to raise the militia to defend London is unknown, although they would have included Middlesex, which contains no other *burh*. Essex in the late ninth century would have been Viking territory, while to the north of Middlesex the men of Hertfordshire would have been concerned with the defence of Hertford. It has been suggested that the estates known as *Basingahaga* and *Staeningahaga* give a clue to the source of militia, since they preserve the names of two estates, Basing and Staines, which lie on the Roman road to Silchester (Dyson and Schofield 1984, 306–7). Both are apparent examples of the contributory manors known from the Domesday survey to have been attached to many boroughs. There is no evidence that military service was due from such manors in particular (since it was due from every estate) and by the time of Domesday it is more likely that the contributory manors reflect an economic interest in tenth and eleventh-century towns by the holders of rural estates.

By the later tenth century, the defence of London was probably in the hands of its permanent inhabitants who, from the reign of Athelstan at least, had formed a peace-guild whose duties then included administering justice and hunting down miscreants (Whitelock 1968, 387–91). By the

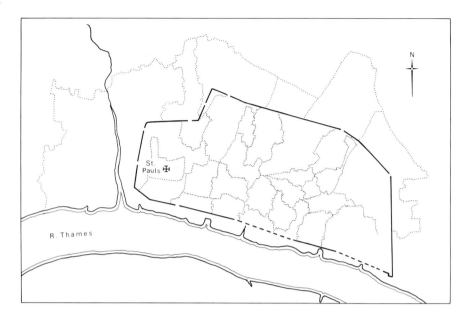

FIG. 46   Ward boundaries in the city of London (after Brooke and Keir). Since the wards were the units used to muster troops in the late Saxon and later times it is likely that a small ward originally held the same number of fighting men as a large one. The boundaries therefore indicate that the area around Cornhill and Gracechurch Street may have been the most populous, whilst some areas just inside the defences were probably very sparsely occupied. This conclusion agrees with the archaeological evidence for the tenth to twelfth centuries.

eleventh century the defence of London was organised by wards. Each ward had an alderman who was responsible for mustering a quota of men and each ward had a particular stretch of wall or gate to man. The ward boundaries survive and show that they varied in size, presumably because of differences in the density of occupation (*see* Fig. 46). The ward system may have been in existence in London from the ninth century or, and this is more likely, London may originally have been defended by rural militia who were replaced by Londoners as the population of London grew.

To summarise, it is clear that little is known about the defence of London during the mid-Saxon period. It seems to have lost any function as a fortress during the fifth to ninth centuries, although it was probably used as a refuge. In the ninth century London became a garrisoned fortress and the walls again became important. We may expect that minor repair works and ditch digging took place but there is no archaeological evidence for the condition of the walls themselves. The lower courses of the Roman wall must have stood, since they were used as the foundation for later medieval rebuilding. The first archaeological evidence for a ditch can be dated to the mid-eleventh-century, but we cannot yet tell to which side of the Norman conquest it belongs.

8 Trade

The primary reason for the existence of a settlement at London in the mid-Saxon period was trade. So far as we know, the administration of the surrounding district, the religious needs and the defence of the local population all took place through other means. It is therefore important that the actual evidence for trade is carefully examined.

Ideally, historians and archaeologists would like to be able to talk quantitatively about trade. What was the volume or value of goods shipped through London? What was the balance of trade? How did these figures vary through time and between regions? Unfortunately, the means to answer these questions are not available. Many of the likely items of trade have left no archaeological record nor are they adequately recorded in documents. A prime example is the trade in slaves. The Anglo-Saxon slave trade is only recorded incidentally in the late sixth century because Pope Gregory ordered the purchase of English (Northumbrian) slaves to be trained as missionaries and sent back to England to help in the conversion (Whitelock 1968, 606, 687, 727). The origin of this trade is unknown but Bede shows, again incidentally, that Frisian slave-traders were in London in the late seventh century (Whitelock 1968, 661). Slaving was still practised in England in the eleventh century – Bishop Wulfstan preached against the Dublin-Bristol trade in the early eleventh century – but there is no indication of its importance. In 1036 one of the sons of King Ethelred the Unready, the *aetheling* (Prince) Alfred, returned from exile in France. Some of his men were captured in Guildford and sold as slaves (Whitelock 1968, 323). Slaves, *servi*, were still a common class in the Domesday Book in some regions of England in 1086.

Other potential exports, such as grain, wool or cloth, should be fractionally easier to detect archaeologically and there is less reason for their not being mentioned in contemporary documents. However, there are problems in the characterisation of such goods. It is not uncommon to find cereal grains on archaeological sites, mainly preserved by charring, but there is no difference between grains of cereals grown in England and those on the Continent. Occasionally a deposit may be found in which the weeds harvested with the grain are also present. Analysis of such weeds can sometimes identify a deposit as an import, as has been done for an early Roman cache from the site of the forum in London, but this depends on the grain being exported to a region with a substantially different climate.

Livestock trade is equally difficult to document. There is a reference in an eleventh-century document to what may be the export of live pigs from London, although the Latin could signify bacon. How such a trade could be demonstrated archaeologically is difficult to imagine. What we find is the rural estate where the animals were reared, a network of roads and tracks leading to London and facilities for breaching and loading ships. If animals were slaughtered in London and their carcasses exported we might hope to find animal bone evidence for the trade, since the extremities without much meat cover – skulls, mandibles and feet bones – would be discarded close to the butchery. Studies of the animal bones from Saxon sites in the London area are under way at present but the only one to be published is that of the late mid-Saxon material from the Treasury, Whitehall (Chaplin 1971, 124–138). The overall ratio of meat bones by weight from the site showed that cattle were far and away the most important source of meat consumed, with sheep and pigs an equal second. Horse, dog, deer and bird were very badly represented and were obviously not regularly consumed. The majority of the cattle were mature and could therefore have been driven to London. The ratio of humerus and femur fragments to mandibles shows that only about one half of the cattle slaughtered on the site were eaten there, a similar ratio to that found for sheep. About 10 per cent of the sheep bones came from very young sheep, not likely to have been driven to London. They show that flocks were kept in the settlement. A further 30 per cent of the sheep were killed before maturing and were therefore probably kept for meat rather than wool, but 60 per cent were mature and presumably only killed after they had produced several fleeces. Pigs, by contrast, show no sign of having been slaughtered for export and since 40 per cent were killed in their first year they were probably kept on the site. The absence of mature pig bones could either mean that few reached maturity or that live pigs (or complete carcasses) were exported from mid-Saxon London.

Studies in Denmark have shown that there is a difference between urban and rural bone assemblages (Randsborg 1980, 54–7). The former have a higher proportion of pig bones, presumably because pigs could be kept in cramped conditions or turned out to forage, while sheep and cattle had more specialised requirements. Place-name evidence shows that a number of places along the Thames have the element -*hythe*, meaning wharf or landing place (Chelsea, Erith, Lambeth, Maidenhead, Putney and Stepney). Amongst them was Rotherhithe, first recorded in the eleventh century. The first element of this name comes from the Anglo-Saxon word for cattle. The cattle may have been simply ferried across the river to London rather than being exported, however. A similar problem exists for the name Lambeth, 'Lambhythe', recorded in 1042 as the location of the hall in which Harthacnut died. There was a ferry across to Westminster at Lambeth, probably from the mid-Saxon period onwards.

Wool is another commodity which is likely to have been an important element in Saxon trade, either in its raw state or woven into cloth. The wool fibres themselves can be analysed to give some indication of the breed of sheep and the weave of cloth can be classified. There are patterns in the distribution of different weaves which, it is thought, might indicate sources, but these patterns are much too broad for a specifically English cloth to be identified, let alone the products of London looms (Bender-Jorgensen 1986). However, the archaeological study of textiles is in its infancy, owing to the meagre quantity of textile fragments which has been excavated from London and the lack of comparanda. Cloth was almost certainly being made on a large scale in mid-Saxon London, however, since clay loom weights are common finds in the area of the Strand settlement (*see* Fig. 47). Cloth produced by the nuns of Barking was well-known and could have been exported.

Since the major exports from London cannot be studied in detail, through lack of evidence, we must turn to imports. In the late twelfth century Fitzstephen gives a list of the goods entering London, actually a quote from a verse based on Virgil:

Gold from Arabia, from Sabaea spice And incense; from the Scythians arms of steel Well-tempered; oil from the rich groves of palm That spring from the fat lands of Babylon; Fine gems from Nile, from China crimson silks; French wines; and sable, vair and miniver From the far lands where Russ and Norseman dwell.

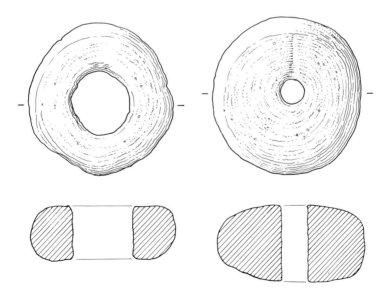

FIG. 47 Typical Saxon loom weights. *Left*: mid-Saxon loom weight from the Strand settlement. *Right*: late Saxon loom weight from the city. (After Wheeler)

He emphasises the exotic and luxury nature of London's imports. Whether this was a true picture and, if so, whether it was equally true during the Saxon period is difficult to tell. Here again, the majority of the imports would leave little trace or cannot be characterised.

There is some evidence for deep-sea fishing, in the form of bones of cod and ling, and for the importation of oysters and other shellfish. A series of iron fish hooks from Billingsgate lorry park, dated to the mid-eleventh century, is further confirmation of the existence of the fishing industry in Saxon London. Preliminary results of the analysis of fish bones from mid-Saxon and late Saxon London show that deep-sea fishing took place in both periods, but that in the mid-Saxon period there was much more use made of the resources of the Thames, especially eels (Locker, forthcoming).

Imported fruits can sometimes be identified by their seeds and both grape and fig seeds have been found in mid-Saxon and Saxo-Norman pits in London. Neither were found in large quantities. Lentils, represented by a charred seed from mid-Saxon London, would probably also have been imported (Davis and de Moulins, forthcoming).

Imported silks have been recognised from tenth-century pits at Milk Street (*see* Fig. 48). Such silks would probably have been used as trimming on woollen garments and as garters and hair nets. A small consignment of silk would, therefore, go a long way (Pritchard 1984, 70).

Artefacts of stone are amongst the best materials for the archaeological study of trade. Stone of different properties was quarried in many parts of the British Isles, Scandinavia and western Europe and can often be identified.

FIG. 48   Part of a strip of silk recovered from a tenth-century pit at Milk Street, London. (Museum of London)

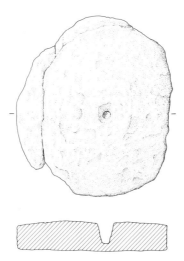

FIG. 49 The lower stone from a Rhenish lava quern found reused in the footings of an eleventh-century building at Pudding Lane, London. (Drawn by Sue Mitford)

The most common stone artefacts were hone stones and querns and both would have been in common use in the Saxon period. Until the use of wind or water-powered mills became standard, every household would have needed a quern to grind corn and every adult would have needed a hone to sharpen weapons or tools. The London area does not contain outcrops of hard rock — although blocks of chert and sarsen stone can be found in the gravels — and the best sharpening stones must not only be hard but fine-grained, so that their use did not produce scratches or burrs on the edge being sharpened. In the Roman period hones were made of Kentish ragstone and a hone made from this stone was found on the mid-Saxon Jubilee Hall site although it could have been a reused Roman one. Sandstone hones were used in the tenth century. From the variety of sources and their appearance it seems that they were made from pebbles picked out of the local gravel. In the eleventh century hones of blue phyllite and, later, Norwegian ragstone are found. Both these stones were quarried in southern Norway and by the thirteenth century Norwegian rag-stone hones were in use throughout England. Evidence from Scandinavia shows that the ragstone was being quarried in the tenth and early eleventh centuries but the earliest examples from London are probably of post-conquest date. Almost all the quernstones known from London were made in the Rhineland from Niedermendig lava. Fragments are known from the Strand in the mid-Saxon period, and from the walled city in the tenth and eleventh centuries (*see* Fig. 49). The importation of querns to London seems to have declined sharply in the twelfth century and by that date, presumably, Londoners were buying ready-milled flour.

The goods described so far were all imported or exported as trade items, but a fundamental problem in the study of Saxon London's role as a port is that if goods were being imported to London it was presumably so that they could be exported again, into the hinterland. Because ships were coming into the port of London it was possible to obtain foreign goods even where local alternatives were available. The most useful of these 'accidental' imports is pottery. Pots in the Anglo-Saxon period were invariably made from local clays and in many cases these clays contain rock fragments or minerals which can be characterised, or 'finger-printed'. London itself is situated close to deposits of London clay, brickearth and terrace gravels. Within a few kilometres of London shelly clays, which could be worked and fired with little preparation, could be obtained. This variety is extremely useful to the archaeologist, since it means that pottery made from clays only a few kilometres apart can often be distinguished.

In the late Roman period the majority of the pottery found in London was made in a few large 'factories'. These were extensive rural areas, normally close to woodland, clay deposits and a means to transport the finished products. Pottery production was an important activity in these regions and there must have been a complex distribution system to market the pots. For London the most important supply areas were all at some distance from the city: at Alice Holt and a wide surrounding area on the border of Hampshire and Surrey, at Much Hadham in Essex, the Oxford area, and the Nene Valley in the East Midlands. A few vessels came from much further afield: two-handled containers, *amphorae*, from North Africa and the eastern Mediterranean testify to the importation of wine, olive oil and other produce (such as fish sauce) into late fourth-century London. A few fine table wares of this late date are known, from eastern Gaul (now Belgium) and North Africa.

This pottery demonstrates that even at the end of the fourth century the trade routes in and out of London were still active. If pottery from the south-east of England, the upper Thames and the East Midlands was coming into London then presumably other goods, of greater economic importance, were too. The presence of Mediterranean *amphorae* is particularly significant since they show that London was still able to receive goods from the other end of the Empire. These late *amphorae* are not usually found on rural sites, although London is by no means the only Romano-British town to have produced them, and this must either mean that the main market for eastern Mediterranean wine and oil was in the towns or that the contents of the *amphorae* were split into smaller units before being sent inland.

In the fifth century the pottery industry in Britain collapsed. It was quite clearly still in existence in the last decade of the fourth century, and there are groups of pottery from the floor of the Billingsgate Bathhouse and the Tower of London which show that pottery was being used and broken in just the same way as it had been throughout the Roman occupation. The collapse seems therefore to have been sudden and could have taken place as early as *c.* 400. The Romano-British at Verulamium do not seem to have used pottery in the early fifth century, while the early Germanic settlers used pottery which seems to have been made in and around their settlements, rather than traded wares. This conclusion may be modified by scientific analysis of early Anglo-Saxon pottery and by studies of the stamps used to decorate it. Both lines of evidence suggest that pottery was not being made within each and every settlement and that there were some specialist potters, even if their products were not traded, or at least not traded in the same way as those of their Romano-British predecessors. A few collections of pottery have been found at sites such as Tottenham Court and Rectory Grove, Clapham, which must belong to the fifth to seventh centuries, although exactly where is unknown (Whytehead and Blackmore 1983, 82; Densem and Seeley 1982, 182−3). The precise source of the vessels used on these sites is not known but there is certainly no indication that the pots were being made outside the lower Thames valley. Contemporary pottery from Mucking is different in fabric, as is pottery from sites on the Thames gravels around Abingdon (Vince 1989). This is, of course, not surprising but when similar comparisons can be made with other sites, closer to London, so the potential source of the London area pottery will be narrowed down.

The pottery from the Strand settlement excavations is still being studied but it is at present thought possible to recognise two phases, perhaps dating to the seventh to eighth centuries and late eighth to ninth centuries respectively. In the earlier phase the majority of the pottery found is similar in appearance to its early Anglo-Saxon antecedents. Some appears to have been made in the London area using a clay rich in brickearth sand, for example the Savoy Palace pot, which can also probably be dated to the seventh century by its form (*see* Fig. 50). However, these pots from the London area are not common; the majority of this early-looking pottery has a fine textured fabric in which numerous minute flecks of white mica are visible. The potters had added quantities of organic material, probably in the form of dung, which gave the fabric a black core and pock-marked surface (*see* Fig. 51). Micaceous clays which could have formed the raw material for this pottery can be found in the highest Tertiary deposits around London, such as those which form Highgate Hill (the Claygate Beds). They are more common, however, in south and central Essex, and were used by medieval potters at Mill Green, Ingatestone, for example. Mid-Saxon organic-tempered pots like those from the Strand have been found at Nazeingbury and Barking Abbey, both in the Roding Valley; it is likely that the Strand vessels were made in south-west Essex.

Found alongside these crude, handmade vessels in the early mid-Saxon phase are sherds of Ipswich-type ware. This kiln-fired pottery, although

FIG. 50   A complete seventh-century pot and four clay loom weights from the site of the Savoy Palace, Strand. (Museum of London)

not made on a wheel, shows signs of rotary finishing, probably on a turntable. Kilns producing the ware have been excavated in Ipswich itself. Ipswich is not mentioned in mid-Saxon documents, nor can its mint signature be found on any coins, but it nevertheless appears to have been an important port, perhaps the major port for the kingdom of East Anglia. A number of the London Ipswich-type ware finds are from large storage jars decorated with stamping on the shoulders which might have been used as containers (perhaps for carrying water on board ship?). Ipswich-type ware is found at sites all along the east coast of England, from Canterbury in the south to the Lincolnshire Fens in the north. It is also found at sites well away from the coast, for example at Aylesbury in Buckinghamshire and Winchcombe in Gloucestershire. It is unlikely that Ipswich-type ware was ever in common use on these inland sites but the very fact of its presence, in contrast to the extremely localised nature of much of the early Anglo-Saxon pottery of south-eastern England, shows that overland travel had become easier during the mid-Saxon period. On the Strand, Ipswich-type ware became the most common pottery type in use, as is shown by the finds from the Treasury, Whitehall.

A few vessels from the Strand are from non-local English sources. A sizeable minority contain a distinctive iron-rich sand which is character-

FIG. 51   A chaff-tempered pot from the London area with (inset) detail of the surface. (Museum of London)

istic of parts of the Lower Greensand, on the border of Surrey and Hampshire and in central Buckinghamshire and south Bedfordshire. There is even one from the East Midlands which contains fragments of igneous rock from the Charnwood Forest, but the most notable finds are imports from the Rhineland and what is now northern France and south-eastern Belgium. A few are of the very distinctive type known as Tating ware which had a burnished black surface onto which was stuck tin foil. This ware, which scientific analysis now suggests was made at more than one site (Hodges 1981, 64–8), can be dated on the Continent to the late eighth and early ninth centuries. The Rhenish pots from the Strand were probably mainly large containers and may have come to London filled with wine. The other vessels often had spouts and seem to have been connected with drinking.

At present too little is known about the precise date of the latest pottery from the Strand settlement to tell whether it is of early, middle or late ninth-century date, nor is it clear whether there was any change in the sources of pottery as a result of the disruption to trade caused by Viking raids and continental political unrest. A handful of sherds of mid-Saxon pottery has been found on sites within the walled city and these are probably contemporary with the Strand settlement, rather than being examples of the pottery used by the first secular inhabitants of the city. The earliest pottery found in late Saxon deposits in the London area is likely to date to the late ninth or early tenth centuries and contrasts strongly with the Strand pottery. There are virtually no imports, no pottery from the Ipswich kilns (which continued in use into the late Saxon period, but producing wheelthrown pottery), and no locally made pottery. Almost all the sherds found are of the same ware, LSS. This shell-tempered ware was made from a Jurassic clay, probably a shelly marl within the Oxford clay. The nearest outcrop of this clay to London is to the west of the Chilterns and a study of the distribution of this ware shows that the pottery mainly becomes less common as one travels away from south-east Oxfordshire, but that there is a second focus, around London (*see* Fig. 52). This suggests that either there were actually two production sites, one in the Oxford region and the other close to London, or that pottery was being sent directly to London and being redistributed from there. Sites on the Thames in Berkshire or Buckinghamshire, such as Wraysbury, have only small quantities of this ware, which probably shows that it was not carried by boat down the Thames but overland, through the Chilterns.

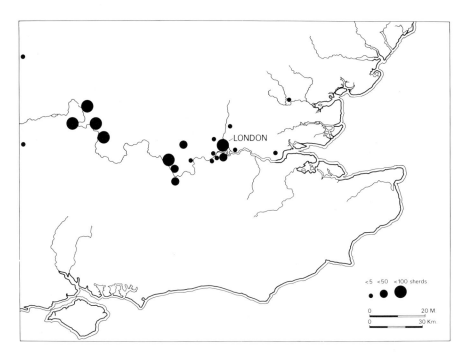

FIG. 52   The distribution of Late Saxon Shelly ware in the Lower Thames Valley. There are sporadic finds of this ware to the north-west of this area and recent work in Oxfordshire has revealed further finds there. Within the Lower Thames Valley all the known findspots are shown.

During the early eleventh century LSS ceased to be traded to London and in its place a number of wares are found. The date of this change can be quite accurately estimated through the dendrochronological dating of the Billingsgate waterfronts. Successive deposits were datable to *c.* 1040, *c.* 1055, *c.* 1080 or later and *c.* 1108 or later. In the first deposit LSS was still the most common ware found, although new, more local wares and imports were present. In the succeeding group LSS had disappeared and the most common ware found contained iron-rich sand identical to that found in some of the mid-Saxon wares from the Strand. In the latest groups sherds of pottery made in London or its immediate surroundings were found.

The local wares which replaced LSS came from a number of sources. By comparing their fabrics with those of wares from sites in north Kent, north Surrey, Middlesex and Essex we can show that the first wares came from north Kent and the south bank of the Thames. Later, wares from the Surrey-Hampshire border from Hertfordshire or Buckinghamshire, the Hertfordshire-Middlesex border and south Essex are also found. The strong Essex connection postulated in the mid-Saxon period is not seen at this time and the south Essex wares are uncommon. The imported vessels found in these groups also change with time. The earliest and always the most common vessels came from the Rhineland, while the later groups produced odd sherds of northern French pottery, from two or three separate sources, and sherds of Andenne-type ware from the Meuse valley.

The archaeological evidence for trade is therefore based on what were undoubtedly insignificant items – stone querns, honestones and pottery – some of which were probably not imported as direct trade goods anyway. Nevertheless, Ethelred's fourth law code contains a list of merchants having rights in London which agrees quite well with the archaeological evidence (*see* Fig. 53). The Danes had many privileges in London, but their presence as traders is difficult to document archae-ologically, apart from the few honestones. The remaining merchants came from the Rhineland, the Meuse Valley and northern France. Wine appears to have been one of the main goods imported from these areas and a few wine barrels have been found in the walled city, reused as the linings for wells. They have the same long narrow profile as those to be seen in the Bayeux Tapestry being loaded aboard ship and containing provisions for William's invasion force.

The historical evidence for trade has been alluded to above and, indeed, the majority of references to London before the 880s are to a greater or lesser extent concerned with trade. Bede's account of the Frisian slave-trader and Ethelred's fourth law code give specific examples of foreign traders in London, in the seventh and the eleventh centuries. Other

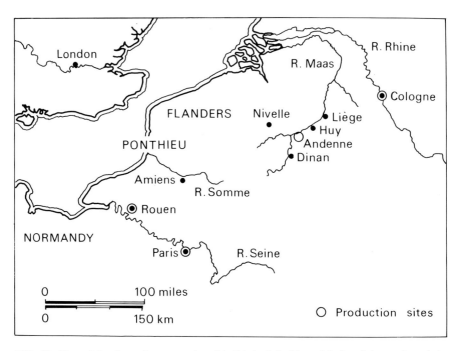

FIG. 53 The origin of merchants mentioned in Ethelred the Unready's fourth law code and the sources of continental pottery imported to London in the eleventh century.

references do not tell us who carried out the trade but nevertheless reinforce its importance. The earliest references to trade in London are a charter of Frithuwold, sub-king of Surrey, who gave land near the port of London in a charter dated between 672 and 674 (Whitelock 1968, No. 54; Dyson 1980; Biddle 1984). The laws of Hlothere and Eadric of Kent, issued between 673 and 685, have a section dealing with men of Kent who buy property in London. The laws show that the kings of Kent had a London official, a *wic-reeve*, whose duty it was to witness transactions at the king's hall. In the early 730s, when Bede described London as part of his account of the foundation of St Paul's, he called it 'situated on the bank of the aforesaid river (Thames), and a mart of many nations coming to it by land and sea' (Whitelock 1968, No. 151, 169). His text uses the present tense at this point and it could well be that Bede was describing contemporary, early eighth-century London for the benefit of his Northumbrian readers. It is important to note that Bede mentions both land and sea, since this is one more piece of evidence which suggests that the road network leading in and out of London was current in Bede's day, if not in 604.

At the same time as Bede was writing his history Aethelbald of Mercia was granting remission of toll on ships using the port of London to various religious institutions, of which records survive for Worcester,

Rochester, Minster in Thanet and St Paul's. In one such grant he states that the toll belonged to the king by royal right (Whitelock 1968, No. 66, 452). These grants were still current over a century later and one from Rochester was confirmed *c.* 844−5 by Brihtwulf of Mercia. Later still, in 857, Burgred of Mercia granted the liberty of the estate of *Ceolmundinghaga* to the Bishop of Worcester 'with all the things which rightly belong to it, great and small, *i.e.* that he is to have therein to use freely the scale and weights and measures as is customary in the port' (Whitelock 1968, No. 92, 487−8). There is no clear evidence from this grant as to whether the estate was inside or outside of the west gate, but the tenor of the grant is that it was an urban estate, acquired for the purposes of commerce. Similar clauses can be found in the Queenhithe charters of 888/9 and 898/9 (Dyson 1978, 205). The second of these charters refers to Queenhithe which, to judge by its original name of Ethelred's hithe, was an official harbour. In the first charter King Alfred and Ealdorman Ethelred retained the right to trade on the *ripa emptoralis*, but in the second both recipients were allowed to moor ships along the width of their estates. No excavation along the waterfront has found any evidence for activity at this early date and the balance of probability is that the Queenhithe area, which has not been excavated, was the main and possibly the only area along the waterfront where trade was permitted until the late tenth or even early eleventh century.

References to London in the early to mid-tenth century are few and far between, yet in the reign of Athelstan (924−940) London was assigned eight moneyers, the highest number in the country. The *Ordinances of the Bishops and Reeves of London*, written in Athelstan's reign, make no mention of trade, although this is probably because they are concerned only with peace-keeping in the rural districts administered from London (Whitelock 1968, No. 37, 387−391). By contrast, Ethelred's fourth law code, which as noted before (*see* pages 34−5) cannot be precisely dated but is certainly pre-conquest, is remarkably detailed. It contains the first record of Billingsgate which, with Queenhithe and Dowgate, formed the three public wharves of London, and lists the conditions under which foreign merchants were allowed to trade in London.

The many archaeological observations along the city waterfront, from Baynard's Castle in the west to the Custom House in the east, show that for most of its length the Thames lapped up against the riverside wall at high tide. Only in the eastern half of the city, between Dowgate and Billingsgate, were artificial arrangements made to allow boats to be unloaded (*see* pages 33−4), and then only in the eleventh century.

The general pattern of the ebb and flow of trade is quite clear from both archaeological and historical evidence. In the late Roman period London still had direct contact with the Mediterranean world, and was connected to the countryside by a road network whose use is shown by the distribution of pottery. Early in the fifth century this trade ceased, although whether this was a result of the depopulation of the city or perhaps one of its causes is unknown. By the middle of the seventh century the Strand settlement was in existence as an international trading centre. We are still lacking knowledge of its origins but the concentration of early mid-Saxon finds around Charing Cross — Drury Lane, Maiden Lane, Jubilee Hall, the Savoy Palace — suggests that it began as a relatively small settlement and grew westwards to Whitehall and eastwards to the Fleet during the eighth century. This is good evidence that the trade passing through London was growing during this period.

The inability to find mid-ninth-century or later occupation either in the Strand area or in the walled city suggests that the trade through London must have declined if not stopped altogether. This can only be a tentative conclusion at present, since it is possible that it is our inability to date pottery and other finds of this period with precision which is responsible for the lack of data. Even when we can date occupation, however, there is very little evidence for international trade, or even for coastal trade with East Anglia, which in the ninth century must have been an important trading partner to account for the large proportion that Ipswich-type ware takes up of the latest mid-Saxon pottery from the Strand. The re-emergence of evidence for international trade is firmly within the eleventh century. The first bank along the foreshore at Billingsgate lorry park is dated to *c.* 1040, although there may be slightly earlier activity at the adjoining site of New Fresh Wharf. Ethelred's fourth law code is eleventh century in date and the first appearance of imported pottery in any quantity in the walled city was during the eleventh century. There can be no doubt that international trade in London during the middle of the eleventh century was booming. What remains to be established is just how severe the late ninth and tenth-century recession was and what is the significance of Athelstan's allocation of eight moneyers to London.

A few general points can be made from the archaeological evidence for trade. First, the mid-Saxon and eleventh-century pottery evidence shows a similar pattern. London was in contact with what are now the Rhineland, Belgium and northern France. There were also coastal contacts, with East Anglia, and overland contacts with the Surrey-Hampshire border and the East Midlands. Contact with Kent, demonstrated by Aethelbald's grants to Minster and Rochester, may be reflected in the mid-Saxon pottery but we have too little comparative material from Kent to tell. The only published collection of mid-Saxon pottery from the kingdom is from Canterbury. In the eleventh century a Kentish connection with London is demonstrated by some of the shelly ware (a type known as EMSH) although this is probably from north-west Kent. In between these two very similar patterns is that of the late ninth to early eleventh centuries, when almost all the pottery found in London was being made in Oxfordshire.

Second, even in the eleventh century all trade routes were less sophisti-
cated than in the late Roman period, when goods were reaching the city
overland, around the coast from Dorset and the north-east of England as
well as from the eastern Mediterranean. All this at a time when it might
be suggested that Britain was becoming more isolated from the rest of the
Empire and when towns were certainly different in character from their
early Roman predecessors. The effectiveness of London as a port can also
be seen by looking at its hinterland. Here too pottery is the best source of
evidence. The majority of mid-Saxon pottery from sites in the Thames
valley, from Staines to Barking, is of local manufacture, but Ipswich-type
ware is found in increasing quantities as one travels east. Barking, for
example, may well prove to have as high a proportion of Ipswich-type
ware as the Strand, if the preliminary results of recent excavations are
confirmed (*see* Fig. 54). Sherds of imported pottery too are not restricted
to London and have been found at Old Windsor and Waltham Abbey.
Equivalent imports of eleventh-century date are also found in small
quantities at small urban and rural sites in London's hinterland, such as
Staines.

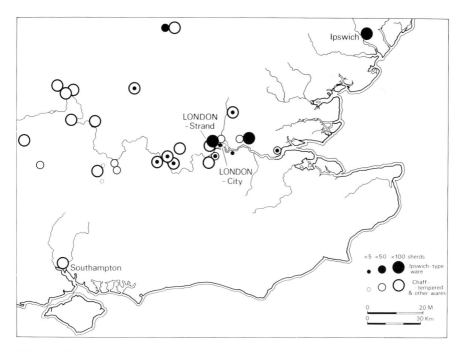

FIG. 54 The distribution of Ipswich-type ware and chaff-tempered ware in the Lower Thames
Valley. Ipswich-type ware has a large coastal distribution (for example, in sites on the Kent
coast) and is widely found in East Anglia. In the Thames valley, however, it is only found in
quantity at the Strand settlement and at Barking Abbey. Away from these centres it is likely that
crude chaff-tempered and other wares continued to be used.

While it would be rash to use this evidence to show that foreign goods were readily accessible in rural England at times in the Saxon period, it is only reasonable to use the same criteria for all periods. We still cannot say to what extent Romano-Britons or Saxons were self-sufficient but we can say that the archaeological evidence for international trade is as strong in the mid-Saxon period as it is in the eleventh century. In order to get another perspective on the economy we must look at the evidence for London as a mint.

9 London as a mint

Until the beginning of the seventh century the Anglo-Saxons lived in a society where coins were not used, although their neighbours across the Channel, in Merovingian France, continued to use and mint coins throughout the fifth and sixth centuries. Continental coins are sometimes found in excavations of Anglo-Saxon sites but these are exceedingly rare and often set for use as jewellery, like the coin of Theodosius (408–50) used in a gold ring found at George Street, Euston Square (Whytehead and Blackmore 1983, 84). In a similar manner, a Byzantine marriage disk of the late sixth or seventh century was cut up and reused to make a pair of earrings, found at Cow Cross near Farringdon Road station (Allason-Jones, forthcoming) (*see* Fig. 55). Coins at this period were certainly valued but it is extremely unlikely that they were used as a medium of exchange since they seem to have been both too rare and too precious.

The first coins to be used for exchange after the Roman period were Merovingian *tremisses*. These gold pieces are also exceedingly rare but

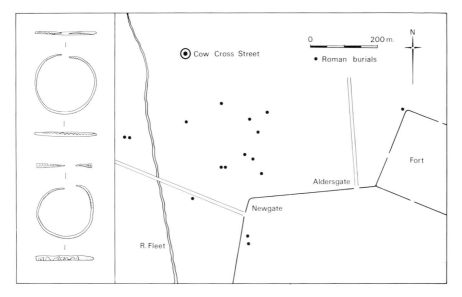

FIG. 55 The Cow Cross earrings are made out of a sixth-century gold Byzantine marriage disk. They probably came from a rich burial of the sixth or seventh century, but whether there was any connection between this burial and the late Roman cemetery at Smithfield is doubtful.

one has been found on the Thames foreshore at Blackfriars. Unfortunately, the foreshore there was formed in the late seventeenth century and therefore the coin must have been dumped with building refuse, presumably from within the walled city. Another coin was found at Pinner, in north Middlesex, but we have no knowledge of its archaeological context. This part of Middlesex is thought to have been wooded during the mid-Saxon period, forming part of Harrow Weald, but the area would have been used for hunting by the nobility and travellers would have had to cross it to reach the Chilterns. Of course, like all stray finds, these two coins could have been brought into the country at a much later date, as a sixth-century coin of Justinian found on the site of a medieval inn in Southwark almost certainly was. Nevertheless, Stuart Rigold amassed a long list of continental *tremisses* as part of his study of the coin hoard found in the Sutton Hoo ship burial and the majority are probably genuine finds (Rigold 1973, 653−77). It is probably such coins which were the basis for the reckoning used by Aethelbert of Kent in his law code. To lie with a *ceorl's* serving woman, for example, entailed six shillings compensation while the same act with a slave-woman of the second class would result in fifty *sceattas* compensation (Whitelock 1968, No. 29, 358). Whether such compensation was actually paid in cash is less certain, although Law Thirty states that if anyone killed a man, he was to pay with his own money and unblemished goods, whatever their kind. A monetary value was placed upon all manner of injuries and a fixed scale of compensation for murder, dependent on the class of the victim, was decreed.

From these laws we can see that coinage found a non-commercial use in the early seventh century. The Sutton Hoo hoard emphasises the symbolic nature of this early use of coins, since the coins seem to have been carefully selected and were certainly not a typical sample of coinage drawn out of circulation. Nevertheless, by the middle of the century coins, known as *thrymsas*, were being minted in England in large enough quantities to require the use of multiple dies of the same design. This coinage would be virtually unknown without the evidence of a single hoard, found at Crondall on the border of Surrey and Hampshire. We are lacking an adequate description of the discovery which, like the Sutton Hoo hoard, may have been a symbolic deposit rather than connected with commerce.

Some of the coins in this hoard have a mint mark for London on them, although they do not bear the name of the issuing authority (*see* Fig. 56). The dating of these coins depends to a large extent upon their composition. A study of Merovingian coins, which bear the names of their issuers and can be dated, shows that in the late sixth century they contained a high proportion of gold − 90 per cent, in fact as pure as could be obtained at the time. During the seventh century there was a consistent and rapid decline in the gold content, silver being added to make up the difference.

FIG. 56 A gold *thrymsa* minted in London. (Photograph of an electrotype in the British Museum)

Analysis of the English coins shows that they too vary considerably in gold content; it seems that the gold standard on this side of the Channel kept in line with that operating in Frankia. The English coinage can therefore be placed in a relative order and perhaps even dated by determining its gold content. On these grounds the Crondall hoard seems to date to the middle of the seventh century, *c*. 640. By the number of die-links present it is reckoned that the coins of the London mint in the hoard were quite new when deposited and only one earlier London coin can be postulated. This piece, now in America, bears an inscription which Sutherland interpreted as meaning that it was minted by Eadbald of Kent (616–640) in London (Stewart 1978, 147 and n. 34). If so, its 70 per cent gold content would imply a minting date of *c*. 630.

The discovery of one of the London coins in the Pas-de-Calais suggests that they may well have been used for commerce, and the distribution of stray finds, whatever their mint, should give an indication of the extent of the monetary economy. It shows a concentration in south-east England, mainly Kent but including Essex, Middlesex and East Anglia. Mercia in the mid-seventh century seems to have been outside the circulation area of these coins or, given the rarity of the finds, may just have been poorer.

The absence of many more gold coins with the London mint mark suggests that minting may have been short-lived, but there are suggestions that some of the latest gold coins, in which the gold content was minor or even non-existent, were minted in London (Grierson and Blackburn 1986, 164). From these coins there is a tenuous typological link with some of the earliest pure silver coins, the Series B *sceattas*. These coins too may have been minted in London and examples have been found over a wide area. The use of coins had spread from the south-east by this time and both Wessex and Mercia were included in the coin-using region. Early in the eighth century copper began to be added to the silver coinage until by the middle of the century it sometimes contains virtually no silver at all. Paradoxically, this is actually a good indication that the coins were being used as a true currency, since their value lies not in their metal content but in the faith which their users place in their ability to exchange them for useful goods. These secondary *sceattas* were used over much of England south of the Humber, although they are still much rarer in the north and west than in the south and east. It is to this period that the most common London *sceattas* (Series L) belong.

By this time some regional currencies had developed. A distinctive type is found mainly in Wessex, for example (Series H), and another is mostly found in East Anglia. But the London coins do not belong to this class and are found throughout the coin-using region. The Series B coins are even found on the Continent, mainly at coastal sites, but only one of the later London coins has been found across the Channel, at Domburg at the mouth of the Rhine. Here too the immediate conclusion, that since the eighth-century coins did not circulate as widely there must have been a decline in trade, is probably wrong. What may have happened is that currency areas developed and that whereas London coins were accepted throughout England south of the Humber, because of the political supremacy of the Mercians at this time, they were, for political reasons, not legal tender on the Continent. The development of regional currencies therefore must mean that there was currency circulating within the kingdoms of Wessex and East Anglia, and that money was not just used for dealing with foreign merchants. Be that as it may, there are numerous coins in England for which a Frisian source is postulated (Series E) as well as some which are either Danish or were copying a Danish style (Series W). An alternative explanation of the failure of the Series H and Series R coinages to travel would be that the distributions of their findspots really does mark the limit of the hinterlands of Southampton and Ipswich. If this was the case the London coins would indicate a supra-regional trade through London. Unfortunately there are very few hoards of *sceattas* and therefore very little chance to examine their circulation in detail.

One can make rough calculations of the relative importance of the London mint during the seventh and eighth centuries, but these can only be translated with extreme caution into the relative volume of trade flowing through the minting places, since the siting of a mint at London rather than, say, Rochester was probably a political as well as an economic act. There is a school of thought which suggests that the absence of a king's name from the *sceatta* coinage implies that it was not issued under royal control but this conflicts with the obvious interest of the king in the toll collected at ports such as London. In the gold coinage period London appears to be less productive than Kent, but was the only regular mint outside that kingdom (rare coins which may be of West Saxon and Northumbrian origin are known). Coins possibly minted in London account for just over a third of the total known in the later seventh century and form 11 per cent of the total in the early to mid-eighth century. An added difficulty here is that the period of use of many of these coins is imperfectly known and that whereas most of the secondary *sceattas* thought to be of Kentish origin have a respectable silver content, those of Series L do not and could therefore be later (figures based on data in Metcalf and Rigold 1984, 245−68). There does appear to be a period in the early eighth century when the London mint was inactive. Many of the non-London *sceattas* found in the London area probably arrived during this period.

In the late eighth century there was a change in minting practice from the use of thick coins, formed by squashing a lump of metal between the dies, to the use of thin coins stamped out of a sheet. The latter are termed pennies and were first produced by Offa of Mercia. Few coins were given a mint signature and it is a matter of numismatic judgement which coins were minted where. The current view is that London was an important mint for Offa, and for Eadberht, Bishop of London, whom Offa wished to have raised to the status of an archbishop (Metcalf 1974, 213−4; Stewart 1986, 27−44). It continued to be a mint for Offa's successors, although throughout this period it only produced a small proportion of the total coins known. Of those coins recorded by 1963, 9 per cent of those minted between 796 and 820 were from the London mint, 8 per cent of those minted in 821, none of those minted in 823 and 14 per cent of those minted between 825 and 840 (Blunt *et al* 1964). During this period, Egbert of Wessex issued a coin at London, giving the mint mark prominence on the reverse (*see* Fig. 57). This issue, known only from a single coin, was probably minted to celebrate the capture of London from the Mercians in 829 and since only one example of this type is known it is unlikely to have been a regular issue. A hoard found at the Middle Temple gives an indication of the coinage circulating in London itself in the 840s (*see* Fig. 58). Of particular interest is the high proportion of coins from East Anglia.

The London mint may have become more important in the reign of Burgred (852−874) and a lead weight found at St Paul's churchyard is stamped with dies of the moneyer Ealdulf for Alfred (*see* Fig. 59). Ealdulf had previously minted for Burgred and the implication of this find is that not only was Burgred's mint in London but that at least one of its Mercian moneyers survived. The exact use of the weight is unknown but it weighs 163.1 grammes, close to half a Roman pound and the weight of

FIG. 57 A penny of Egbert of Wessex, probably minted in 829 to celebrate the capture of London from the Mercians. (British Museum)

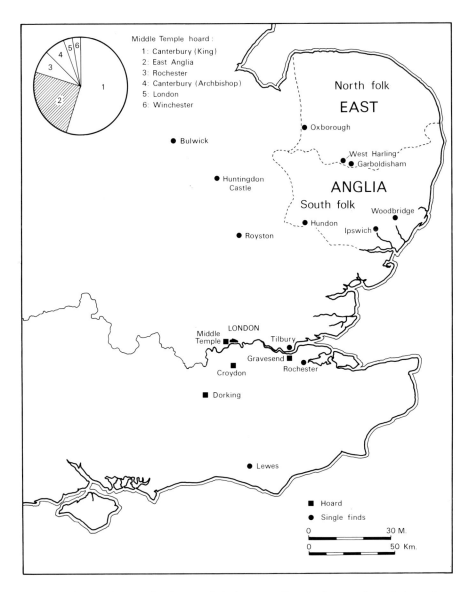

FIG. 58 The distribution of early to mid ninth-century East Anglian pennies and, inset, the composition of the Middle Temple hoard, *c.* 840. (Information supplied by Marion Archibald, British Museum.) The boundaries of the East Anglian kingdom are only approximate.

120 pennies (Archibald 1989). In between the mint of Burgred and that of Alfred was the reign of Ceolwulf II (874–883?). Only a handful of coins are known from his reign, although the similarity in style has suggested that he shared a mint, possibly London, with Alfred, whose early issues are equally scarce. Nevertheless, the absence of evidence for a break in minting, tenuous as it is, is still important when considering the decline of

FIG. 59 A lead weight found at St Paul's churchyard and now in the British Museum. The weight is stamped with official coin dies of Alfred of Wessex but its precise function is uncertain. (Illustration after the Victoria County History)

the Strand settlement and the occupation of the walled city. The importance of the London mint in the late ninth and early tenth centuries is unclear. One of Alfred's issues has a monogram of London on its reverse. This issue is said to commemorate the occupation of London in 886 and, surprisingly perhaps, was often copied by the Vikings of the Danelaw. With this exception and a few special issues, such as that minted at Gloucester, the coins of Alfred and Edward the Elder do not have mint marks.

We do not know whether the ninth-century practice of limiting minting to a few places was continued or whether, as part of the establishment of the *burhs*, minting was de-centralised. The first indication that we have is in Athelstan's Grately decrees:

> 14. Concerning moneyers. Thirdly that there is to be one coinage over all the king's dominion, and no one is to mint money except in a town.
> 14.2. In Canterbury seven moneyers; four of the king, two of the bishop, one of the abbot; in Rochester three, two of the king, one of the bishop; in London eight; in Winchester six; in Lewes two; at Exeter two; at Shaftesbury two; otherwise in the other boroughs one. (Whitelock 1968, No. 35, 384).

Canterbury, Rochester, London and Winchester had all been mints in the ninth century and their pre-eminence in Athelstan's laws may be partly because they were the traditional mints. They are also, however, the most likely points of entry for foreign coins or bullion into England outside the Danelaw. Lewes, Exeter and Shaftesbury were also better placed for overseas contact than, say, Bath or Wallingford or Oxford.

In 973 Edgar reformed the coinage, giving coins a six-year period of use after which they were no longer legal tender. The success of this policy in southern and eastern England can be seen by the number of hoards found containing only one or two issues. From the reform onwards each coin is marked with the moneyer and mint. Study of late tenth and eleventh-century coinage can therefore be undertaken with relative ease, but unfortunately the interpretation of results is difficult. In the late tenth century Ethelred the Unready started to pay tribute to the Danes and vast quantities of English coins have been found in Scandinavian hoards. In these hoards, as in contemporary English hoards, coins from the London mint predominate. An examination of the names of moneyers shows that the increased production needed to supply the Danegeld led to an increase in the number of moneyers at each mint. This increase is noticeable from the second issue of Ethelred II to the first of Edward the Confessor and makes the study of commercial minting more difficult. That there was a tremendous local circulation of coin has been elegantly demonstrated by D. Metcalf of the Ashmolean Museum who compared the composition of a late tenth-century hoard from Chester with the overall incidence of known coins during the same period. The two sets of figures were almost identical, showing that during its six years of circulation the coinage had become so mixed that there was little regional difference in the origin of coins (Metcalf 1978, 168 and Table D). Coins had managed to reach Chester from mints at Canterbury and Totnes within two years of minting.

There is little evidence for the location of the London mint at any period. The lead weight from St Paul's churchyard is perhaps more likely to be an official market weight than one used in the mint itself. At Winchester in the late eleventh and twelfth centuries it seems that the mint was situated in the High Street, immediately outside the king's palace (Biddle 1976, 397−400). From the late ninth century the mint would have been within the walled city, but it could have been anywhere. It may be that minting was dispersed within the town, as other industries seem to have been until the later twelfth century, and the evidence from Coppergate in York may be relevant in this context since a coin die has been found there in a typical urban tenement (Hall 1984, 61). Whether the ninth-century and earlier mint was in the Strand or the walled city is also unknown, although it is likely that Burgred's mint would have been within the walled city even if the *sceatta* mint (or mints) was outside.

By the time of the Domesday Book all moneyers working in England had to send to London to exchange their old dies for new ones. Analysis of the style and lettering on coins shows that up to and including the reign of Cnut regional die-cutting centres existed while some time after that, possibly during the reign of Edward the Confessor, this activity had been centralised at London.

Mention must be made of a small number of lead pieces stamped with official coin dies but not apparently either counterfeit coins or 'trial pieces'. One of Edward the Confessor was found on a site just outside Aldersgate (*see* Fig. 60). A group, dating to the reign of William I, was found at Billingsgate lorry park, discarded on the foreshore in front of the waterfront constructed *c.* 1055 and many more, dating from the reign of Edward the Confessor down to that of Henry I, were found during and after the excavation in spoil from the site. Marion Archibald of the British Museum suggests that these pieces were used as proof of payment of toll, which would certainly fit the London findspots (Archibald 1989).

FIG. 60   A lead 'trial piece' of Edward the Confessor found at Aldersgate. (Museum of London)

The study of the London mint, frustratingly inconclusive though it is, does help to clarify the importance of London in the Saxon period. The inception of the mint in the mid-seventh century fits well with other evidence for the growth or origin of the Strand settlement during this period. On any interpretation the *sceatta* coinage shows that London was one of the most prolific mints in the country, although always secondary to Kent. The one time when the mint appears not to follow the archae-ological evidence is in the late eighth and early ninth centuries. It is, however, in the late ninth and tenth centuries that the numismatic evidence is most crucial. First, we need to know the actual relative output of the London mint before Athelstan. Second, we need to know whether the full complement of moneyers allowed by Athelstan were actually working in London and third, and here there seems little chance of progress, we need to know how much of the coinage minted in London was generated by administrative processes, the recycling of coin and bullion collected in tax, for example, how much was generated by regional trade and how much, if any, by international trade.

10 All roads lead to London? Communication

Most Roman towns eventually had an Anglo-Saxon successor, at least by the tenth or eleventh century. A few Roman towns, such as Silchester or Verulamium, depended entirely on road communications and now lie deserted whereas great medieval cities almost invariably lay on a navigable river. The Anglo-Saxon emphasis on water transport must have been even clearer in the mid-Saxon period, when the only large settlements known were international ports. Excavations near Charing Cross have recently found the mid-Saxon waterfront, stabilised by a revetment which has been dated between 680 and 690 by dendrochronology. Excavations along the waterfront between Billingsgate and Dowgate have shown that from the middle of the eleventh century onwards there were sporadic artificial hardstanding areas in front of the riverside wall. Further west there is documentary evidence for the use of the shore at Queenhithe from the end of the ninth century. The use of lesser rivers for transport is shown by the recent dating by dendrochronology to the late Saxon period of a log boat found in the Hackney Marshes. Nevertheless, it is probable that the concentration of attention upon the waterfront and international contacts by archaeologists has lead to an underestimation of the importance of overland transport in the Saxon period.

Opinions as to the importance of roads for long-distance travel in Anglo-Saxon England vary. On the one hand, Bede tells us that early in the seventh century King Edwin of Northumbria:

> took such good care of his people, that in many places where he saw clear springs near the highways, he caused stakes to be fixed, with copper cups hanging on them, for the refreshment of travellers. (Whitelock 1968, No. 151, 620–1).

On the other hand there is so far no known inland *wic* to compare with the Strand settlement, Saxon Southampton, Ipswich and the like. This can be taken to imply that long-distance trade was conducted by ship and boat and had little impact upon those people living in the interior of the country. Good roads were necessary not only for trade but also for administration and warfare. Students of the Viking wars have noted the routes along which the Viking army travelled and the speed at which they moved and have concluded that these armies must have been using the Roman road system. Indeed, many of the trunk routes used today follow Roman alignments and this is often used as evidence that parts of the Roman road network were in use continuously throughout the Anglo-Saxon period.

A study of the road system around London is useful in this debate because here we have an area where the commercial centre moved, from the city to the Strand. If the Roman road system was in use it should one day be possible to see the modifications needed to divert the roads into the new town, although in the ninth century they would themselves have been made redundant following the shift of settlement back into the walled city.

The terminology used in Anglo-Saxon charters makes it clear that in the late Saxon period some roads were thought of as being of special importance. Legally, people using them were under the king's protection and it was prohibited to build closer than two perches to the road. This requirement is recorded in the Nottinghamshire Domesday survey and can be demonstrated to pre-date the Norman conquest, since Abbot Leofstan of St Alban's (1048–66) is recorded as clearing trees to either side of Watling Street, for the safety of travellers to London (VCH Middlesex 1, 97). A restriction on building closer to the king's highway, and probably fear of strangers, meant that settlements were sited either on bypasses or at the end of short roads running perpendicular to the highway. This can be seen clearly along the stretch of Watling Street between Willesden and Elstree. The churches of Kingsbury, Hendon, and Stanmore, which were all probably in existence by the late eleventh century, are set back from Watling Street. The small town of Edgware, however, straddles the road but this settlement was a post-conquest foundation, probably of the twelfth century. Uxbridge, another early Norman foundation, similarly straddles the highway but the situation at Brentford and Staines is more complex. At Brentford the Saxon and later town lies to either side of a road parallel to the Roman road, whose line has been found by excavation further to the north, while at Staines the High Street appears to have been re-colonised in the tenth or early eleventh century, although earlier pottery and ditches have been found south of the street. These settlements, and other similar examples, may have originally developed along 'by-passes' which eventually superseded the original highway. It is probably significant that they are usually settlements which had more than an agricultural function, acting as markets, administrative centres or both.

A glance at a map of central London will confirm that a number of Roman roads are followed by present-day routes. To the east of London the medieval and later road follows the Roman line until it is diverted to the south, to cross the River Lea at Bow. The original crossing was a ford, marked by the place-names of Old Ford and Stratford to either side of the river. Excavations on both sides of the river have confirmed the existence of the road. At Old Ford a settlement thriving to at least the end of the fourth century was found, while the Stratford excavation suggested that the Roman road may have continued in use until the twelfth century, when it was re-sited at the time of the construction of Bow Bridge (Sheldon 1972; Mills 1984, 29: Redknap 1987, 296–7).

The road leading out of Bishopsgate, Ermine Street, was followed by the medieval route until it reached Enfield (which, incidentally, may derive its name from *ean-feld* 'open land where lambs were raised'). Further west, the road out of Aldersgate cannot be traced far to the north and appears, in both the Roman period and later, to be a local route. It has been suggested, however, that Aldersgate was actually a principal entrance to London in the ninth century and later, assuming that Newgate was blocked (Tatton-Brown 1986, 21–30). In this theory, which has no archaeological corroboration at present, the route from High Holborn descended into the Fleet valley, crossed the river and then veered north, through land later occupied by St Bartholomew's Hospital. Ironically, a lane was found during excavations in 1979 conducted by David Bentley for the Museum of London but it can be shown that it is of twelfth-century origin and was probably constructed to allow access to Aldersgate from the Fleet without crossing the hospital precinct. It could, of course, be a diversion of a much earlier route.

The road out of Newgate becomes first High Holborn and then Oxford Street. In the twelfth century it was known as Uxbridge Street, showing that by that time the main route had diverted from its Roman line to cross the Colne at Uxbridge, although the original Roman line continues as a route to Staines. Part of this post-Roman addition passes through the estate of Yeading and is likely to be the *via publica* recorded in a charter for Yeading dated between 716 and 757 (Gelling 1979, No. 198, 97). This charter records that the boundary of the estate ran parallel to the road but two *jugera* to the north. There is a stretch of the parish boundary of Yeading which runs parallel with the Uxbridge road which in turn runs down the centre of the medieval parish (*see* Fig. 61). The Oxford Street stretch of this road was termed a *mickle here path*, 'large army street', in the 959 bounds of the Westminster estate. It is quite common for Roman roads to be called *here path* in late Saxon charters, but whether this just preserves the memory of the Roman legions or whether they were so-called because they were currently used by the army is not known.

At Marble Arch the Roman road forked, with one route leading north along Edgware Road, known in the Saxon period as Watling Street. The *Waeclingas* were the people living in or around *Waeclingacaesta*, alias Verulamium, and the Saxon and later route seems to follow the Roman one all the way to St Albans. Excavations at Edgware, however, have

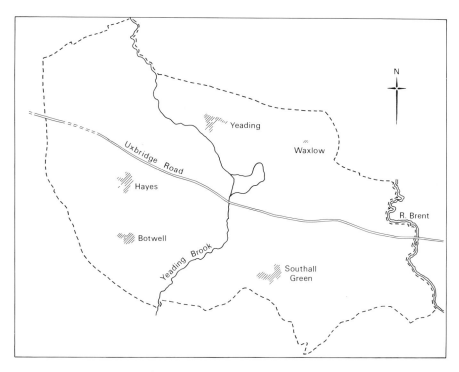

FIG. 61 Saxon estates around Hayes, Middlesex, showing the relationship of Uxbridge road to the northern boundary of Hayes parish. It is suggested here that Uxbridge Road is the *via publica* mentioned in an eighth-century charter because the northern boundary of the Yeading estate lay to the north of it. To the west of the Yeading Brook lay two Anglo-Saxon estates. That of Botwell lay further west than that of the 'lands of the archbishop at Hayes'. These two estates could have formed strips running roughly parallel with the western parish boundary.

shown that the modern road is situated slightly to the east of the Roman line. Branching off Watling Street somewhere in Willesden or Kilburn was another post-Roman street. This one was recorded in the bounds of an estate at Kingsbury in the tenth century and can be seen forming part of the boundary of the medieval parish of Stanmore. The line of the road is then lost but most likely ran to the north-west to cross the Colne at Watford. Only a fragment of this road now survives, as Honeypot Lane, a name which shows that using the road in the late medieval period was like walking in honey. By then it was therefore an unmetalled green lane (*see* Fig. 62). The Kingsbury charter tells us that the road was known in the tenth century as *wic straet*. The term *straet* is usually used of metalled routes, as in Stratford (which occurs as a place-name in Tottenham on the line of Ermine Street as well as on the Mile End road), and it is known that the Saxons made metalled roads, for example on the routes leading into Oxford (Jope 1956, 251).

The name Knightsbridge, first recorded in the reign of Edward the Confessor, shows that a route, important enough to be bridged rather

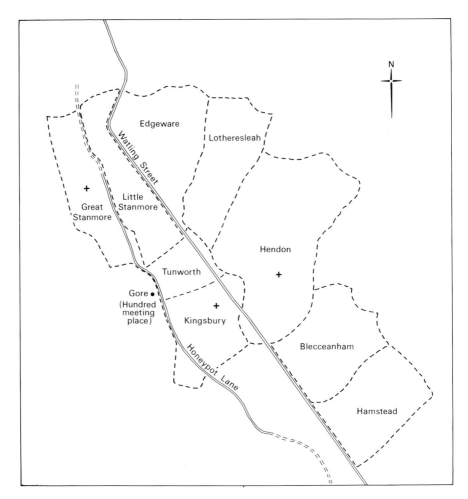

FIG. 62 Saxon estates around Kingsbury, Middlesex, showing the use made of Honeypot Lane as an estate boundary. The lane was an ancient trackway, called *wic straet* in a tenth-century charter.

than forded, crossed the Westbourne at that point. To the east this formed Piccadilly and to the west it split into two roads, leading to Chelsea and Kensington. Both these routes formed parish boundaries for some of their length.

In addition to these known long-distance routes there are a number of places where routes crossed rivers and streams whose existence in the Anglo-Saxon period is recording in place names, for example Greenford which is recorded in 845 and marked a crossing of the River Brent. By the early eighteenth century, when the Rocque map of Middlesex was published, there was no obvious long-distance route crossing the Brent at this point and it is safer to assume that the ford was for local use. Ashford, on the other hand, first recorded in 969, probably took its name from the crossing to be found on the south-west corner of the medieval parish. The boundary at that point followed a road leading from Staines to Hampton, and thence to Kingston, which must therefore be of tenth-century or earlier date.

Further evidence for Saxon routeways comes from a study of medieval parish boundaries. Where Anglo-Saxon charters with bounds exist it can be shown that many of the boundaries that they record survived into the medieval period. Therefore, when there is no contemporary evidence it seems justified to suggest that many of those boundaries too existed in the Anglo-Saxon period. Furthermore, a surprising proportion of the London area parishes consist of rectilinear blocks of land separated by trackways of some sort. Most of these trackways had only local significance in the medieval period but some, especially to the north of London, were part of the series of droveways which led to Smithfield, amongst them the route which gave its name to Holloway.

As these streets, lanes and tracks get closer to London so the route which they followed in the Anglo-Saxon period gets more and more difficult to establish. It can be seen that those from the south converge on a point to the south of Southwark from where they could either head north-east to cross the Thames at Lambeth or north to cross at Southwark. Routes from the east either entered the walled city at Aldgate or detoured north along Old Street to Smithfield. Ermine Street entered the walled city at Bishopsgate and the droveways converged at Islington before heading to Smithfield. Further west, routes joined Oxford Street or fed into the Strand area along the Strand, Piccadilly or Drury Lane. It is likely that all these routes existed in the mid-Saxon period but at present we have no information about when they came into existence. One possibility would be that the routes were in use in the Roman period and never went out of use. Another would be to date them from the laying out of the estates whose boundaries they often formed. That date itself is unknown but is likely to be in the seventh century or earlier (*see* page 133).

The route taken by any of these roads once it reached London is unknown. Within the walled city Fenchurch Street and Lombard Street have the appearance of a convenience route, skirting round the site of the forum, whose courtyard by the mid-Saxon period was probably an overgrown marsh. A shorter route, across Cornhill, can only have come into existence once the west end of the basilica had fallen down, since it cuts across the corners of the building. Excavation has shown that the Roman road north of the basilica was still in use in the fourth century, but that by sometime between the late ninth and the early eleventh centuries properties aligned with Cornhill lay over the demolished walls and floors of the building and ignored the Roman Street. The road through Bishopsgate looks as if it originally veered to the west, along Throgmorton Street, to cross the Walbrook at the same point as Cornhill and Lombard Street and only later was joined by a road leading through the middle of the forum site down to London Bridge. From the Walbrook, crossing Cheapside leads one to the entrance of St Paul's precinct and from there Newgate Street and St Martin-le-Grand lead out through Newgate and Aldersgate. There appears to have been no direct route from the Walbrook crossing to Ludgate, or at least if there was it made no permanent impression upon the city's topography.

In the area of the Strand settlement there is no archaeological evidence for the existence of any streets, but it is more than likely that the Strand itself existed as a riverside road, branching out from the Thames at Charing Cross through Buckingham Palace and the King's Road to Chelsea and Fulham. Piccadilly and Drury Lane, since they are the terminals of long-distance routes of mid-Saxon date, are also likely to have mid-Saxon origins. *Hamwic* and Ipswich both had gridded street patterns in the mid-Saxon period and it is to be expected that London was similar. Observations in service trenches and building sites are being undertaken by the staff of the Museum of London and it is likely that further details of the mid-Saxon street grid will emerge. One factor which suggests that mid-Saxon streets will be found is that the excavations in advance of the National Gallery extension revealed that the whole area had been quarried away during the mid-Saxon period by large gravel pits. These huge features are much bigger than the late medieval pits commonly found on the east side of the walled city and show that some project requiring vast amounts of gravel was undertaken under the control of a central authority (*see* Fig. 63).

It has already been noted that one feature of late Saxon public *burhs* was the provision of a street grid linking the defences to the centre of the settlement. In the walled city there are two areas of regular gridded streets, one to each side of the Walbrook. The western grid is aligned with Cheapside, by far the most important street in that part of the city. When a pipe trench was laid along Queen Street, one of the few major streets in the city not to follow a medieval alignment, it was observed by David Bentley of the Museum of London. This revealed that Cheapside originally extended further south and had a surface of large cobbles. This surface may date to the late ninth century, although no dating evidence was found. By the late eleventh century the southern frontage of Cheapside was approximately on its present line. The north wall of the Norman crypt of St Mary-le-Bow church, however, is set back from this frontage. Perhaps this Norman building replaced an earlier church built to front onto the wider street?

Two streets, Bow Lane and Bread Street, ran south from Cheapside to the Thames, presumably passing through gates in the riverside wall. No other streets run directly from Cheapside to the river, or the riverside wall. No streets ran directly from Cheapside to the northern defences except for Wood Street. This street runs for part of its length

FIG. 63 The National Gallery extension site during excavation, looking south. The large mid-Saxon gravel pits are visible in the foreground. (Museum of London)

over the axis of the Cripplegate fort and might therefore be expected to be an early routeway. However, like many of the streets running off Cheapside to the north, Wood Street appears to be composed of stretches of differing date, the earliest being in the south. Some support for this view comes from excavations at St Alban's House and in the middle of the street at its junction with London Wall. The St Alban's House excavations revealed traces of late Saxon occupation from the late ninth or tenth century onwards, while the latter site showed that the street had shifted somewhat, since underneath twelfth century and later metallings there were remains of timber buildings of the mid to late eleventh century, under which was dark earth. It is likely that the original street grid in the west extended from slightly to the north of Cheapside to the river and from the east end of St Paul's to the Walbrook. Several excavations have confirmed that although some of these streets follow Roman alignments, probably because of the constraints of the surviving Roman features, the majority were laid out over dark earth and bear no relationship to earlier features. At one site, Well Court, the first surfaces of Bow Lane themselves were examined (*see* Fig. 64). The earliest contained a high proportion of reused Roman debris, tile and stone, while its successor was made of gravel. No dating evidence was found within or below the first street, nor in the silt which had accumulated on its surface. The second surface was contemporary with a building which had been occupied in the late ninth to early eleventh centuries and which was probably replaced in the mid-eleventh century. Although not conclusive, these observations suggest that Bow Lane was of late Saxon date. Further evidence for the date of the western street grid comes from the Queenhithe charters, which seem to indicate that the north-south streets which formed the boundaries of the two estates described in the 898/9 document did not exist when one of the estates was first granted in 888/9 (Dyson 1978, 200–215).

FIG. 64 The first surface of Bow Lane, excavated at Well Court. (Museum of London)

To the east of the Walbrook it is possible that the earliest settlement took place along the pre-existing roads of Cornhill and Lombard Street/Fenchurch Street, since there is a concentration of late ninth to mid-tenth century coin finds from that area (*see* Fig. 65). Within the tenth century, however, another street grid was laid out, with its centre at the junction of Fish Street Hill/Gracechurch Street and Eastcheap. Excavations on sites to the north of the bridge have shown that while some of the streets in this area were occupied from the tenth century onwards some were not. Pudding Lane is an example of the latter. It was not possible to excavate underneath the street but pits had been dug up against it from the tenth century onwards. Pudding Lane was certainly of secondary importance to Fish Street Hill and Botolph Lane, both of which seem to have always had buildings fronting them, but it did lead down to the river. The first jetty and hardstanding at New Fresh Wharf, dated by dendrochronology to 971 or later, would have been approached via a gate in the riverside wall from Pudding Lane. A section was dug through Botolph Lane and this managed to demonstrate that the street was laid on a dump of earth which also lay underneath the earliest buildings. The few sherds of pottery found within this dump date it to the late ninth to early eleventh centuries, while the sequence of building levels is long enough to show that the actual date of construction must be towards the beginning of this range.

By a combination of archaeology and study of the earliest accurate map of the eastern grid, surveyed in 1666 after the Great Fire, it is possible to show that the original layout consisted of Eastcheap and a series of north-south streets which run straight down the hill to the riverside wall as well as continuing to the north of Eastcheap. At the southern end of these roads there must have been openings through to the waterfront and, at the south end of Fish Street Hill, onto London Bridge. This grid ran north to meet Lombard Street and Fenchurch Street. On the west it ran to the Walbrook and on the east it ended well before the city wall. The evidence from New Fresh Wharf, however, seems to show that the minor streets which alternate with those like Botolph Lane were in existence by the late tenth century. Their less regular plan could either be due to the fact that they are later than the straight streets or that their position was determined by the inhabitants rather than being surveyed.

At the east end of Eastcheap, until the Great Fire, there was a marked kink at the junction with Tower Street, which runs straight towards the Tower of London. This should date the street to the late eleventh century but, since All Hallows Barking church was in existence before that, there was probably an earlier road giving access to the church.

Excavations along the waterfront have given some idea about the sequence of events and their approximate timing. In the south-west of the city, the riverside wall crumbled into the river in places while in others it was pulled down (since its remains were found toppled northwards).

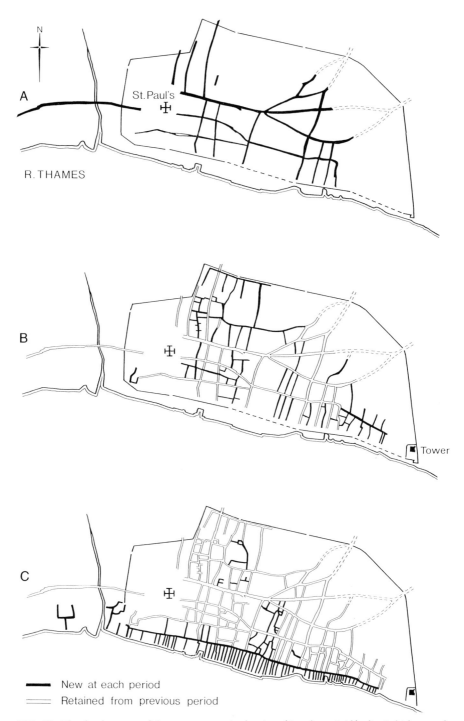

FIG. 65 The development of the street system in the city of London: a) Alfredian?; b) late tenth to late eleventh century; c) later.

A new, timber, waterfront was established immediately, to the south of the Roman wall, and make-up for Thames Street was laid directly on top of the ruins of the wall. At Peter's Hill the north-south street was seen to have been laid down at the same time as Thames Street and a coin of William I was found in its make-up, dating the layout of the street and the destruction of the wall to the post-conquest period. A charter of the Bishop of London dated between 1111 and 1127 records that the chapter built a new wharf on the bare sand at St Paul's Wharf, at the south end of St Benet's Hill (Gibbs 1939, No. 189) and it is likely that by this time the wall had gone and that St Benet's Hill itself was constructed to allow access to the wharf.

During the following centuries, as the land to the south of Thames Street was reclaimed, so lanes were built to serve the new area. Some of these were extensions of lines already existing to the north while others were completely new. The number and density of these lanes shows the pressure for space which had built up within the city and the intensity of the activity down on the waterfront.

In conclusion, it is quite clear that the commonly-held belief that the Saxons relied on Roman roads or dirt tracks is an exaggeration. Not only were old Roman roads kept in use (or perhaps brought back into use) but new ones were created, although their character is difficult to establish. Many still form the arterial routes in and out of London. Some, especially those leading to Smithfield, were probably droveways in the Saxon period as they undoubtedly were later. Those in the walled city were metalled with gravel or cobbles and there is little doubt that streets of a similar nature existed in the Strand area in the eighth and ninth centuries and were supplied with gravel from pits, such as those at the National Gallery extension. In the case of these urban streets there is ample evidence to show that they were constructed to an overall plan, and were probably preceded by a survey (to account for their regular spacing and straightness). Unless a section of one of the rural routes can be excavated there can be no equal certainty that they were in any sense planned, since they could well have become fossilised through use. Perhaps the most difficult features to explain are the tracks which mark the boundaries of Saxon estates. These rarely lead directly to known settlements and can only have arisen after the laying out of the estate if they served an agricultural purpose, moving stock from one area to another for example, or were avoiding the estates. Fieldwork in Essex has shown that similar rectilinear grids arose through the laying out of large tracts of land in the Iron Age and Roman periods. The features there which governed the topography were deep drainage ditches cut into clay. A similar explanation may be responsible for the London area roads, many of which traverse clayland, but this can only be tested through fieldwork.

11 London and the countryside

London sits in the middle of the Thames basin. Essentially, this consists of a large area of clayland, the highest points in which are often capped with gravel. Running through the middle of the basin is the River Thames and on either side of the river are gravel terraces and brickearth. The basin is bounded by chalk hills to the south, west and north-west (*see* Fig. 66).

In the late fourth century the majority of the countryside was intensively cultivated. This can be demonstrated by field survey, in which an area of ploughland is exhaustively walked, the field archaeologist often bent double searching for small scraps of pottery. Such surveys have shown that almost every area examined has a light scatter of fragments of Roman pottery, interspersed with concentrations which mark the sites of former Roman settlements. Such settlements and the fields between them extended from one side of the basin to the other and are found on the

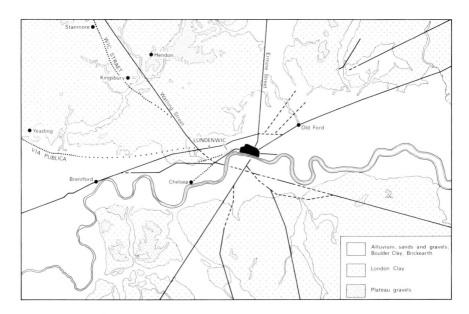

FIG. 66   Roman (black) and later (dotted) roads leading to London.

terrace gravels as well as on the clay. The late Roman landscape surrounding London, as elsewhere on the English clays, seems to have been as fully exploited as their technology would allow. One survey in north-west Essex has indicated that 86 per cent of the settlement sites discovered were occupied in the late fourth century. This is yet one more indication that the economy of Britain on the eve of the fifth century was working at full steam. Until samples of animal bones from these settlements have been studied, together with other environmental studies, it will not be possible to say how much of this late fourth-century population was dependent on selling their crops to survive. If, as one suspects, they were reliant on the cash economy then the sudden collapse of that economy would have had drastic effects on the countryside.

Scattered throughout the claylands, normally straddling the arterial roads, were relatively large rural settlements which seem to have acted as local markets − to judge by the large number of coins found at Old Ford, for example − as well as staging posts and doubtless other official functions. Excavations at Staines, Brentford, Old Ford and Brockley Hill have shown that these sites were abandoned in the early fifth century, like London itself. There is no possibility therefore that the rural economy survived the collapse seen in London, but similarly there is little reason to suppose that the entire population disappeared. The discovery of Roman settlements in areas once covered with woodland, or with place-names which suggest that they were cleared from woodland in the Saxon or medieval period, shows that a certain amount of the clayland reverted to wood but few archaeologists or historians today would suggest that the claylands of the Thames basin were solidly wooded in the Saxon period.

From the middle of the fifth century onwards there is evidence for Germanic settlement in the region, but all of this evidence comes from the gravels and brickearths, none from the clayland. The work of the Museum of London's Department of Greater London Archaeology on the west London gravels is showing that settlement, often amounting to a single hut, extended without a break along the gravels interspersed with areas of prehistoric and Roman field systems which must have still been used in the early Saxon period. Elsewhere the evidence of pagan cemeteries shows that this pattern of extensive but dispersed settlement extended south of the Thames and up the Wandle valley (*see* Fig. 67). The closest evidence to the city of London comes from Rectory Grove, Clapham and Tottenham Court (close to Euston station), both sites thought tentatively to date to the sixth century (*see* Fig. 68). It is possible that the Strand settlement itself has a nucleus of this date around Charing Cross.

Given this wealth of evidence from the gravels it is almost perverse not to accept the implications of the absence of evidence from the claylands. There are sherds of chaff-tempered pottery and burials from Hendon and from Northolt (*see* pages 61−2), both close to medieval churches. The prob-

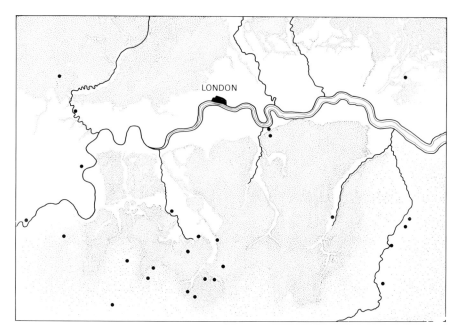

FIG. 67 Early Saxon settlement in the Lower Thames Valley. Note the apparent absence of settlement sites on the brickearths and terrace gravels close to London (shown white).

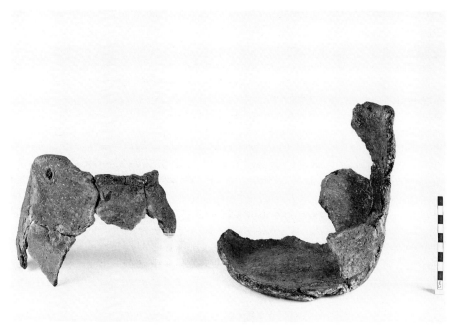

FIG. 68 An early to mid-Saxon pot from Rectory Grove, Clapham. This chaff-tempered vessel had two lugs which could be used with an organic handle, perhaps made of leather or rope. (Museum of London)

ability is that both these sites date to the early mid-Saxon period, between
c. 650 and 750, rather than to the pagan Saxon period. With their exception
there is no evidence at all for early Saxon occupation on the clays. There
are several possible explanations for this pattern. First, the area could
have been part of the British kingdom centred on the Chilterns which was
conquered by the West Saxons in the late sixth century. With this in mind
it is interesting that the only evidence for the date of a post-Roman
settlement on the gravels at Enfield appears to be a bronze buckle (Going
1987). Second, the area could have been exploited by Anglo-Saxons living
around the edges of the claylands. This type of land-use has been postulated
in the Kentish and Sussex Weald. The evidence for this type of land-use
comes from place-names which have forms ending in *-falod* showing that
they were once sheep-rearing pastures, or from charters where rights in
distant woodland are recorded. The absence of such evidence probably
shows that if this sort of land-use was practised on the Middlesex clays it
had been replaced by independent, permanent settlement at a much earlier
date than that in the Weald. Third, it is possible that the difference
between the archaeological evidence from the two subsoils is misleading
and that settlement adapted to a more wooded environment was present
throughout the clayland during the fifth to seventh centuries.

In the seventh century many of the gravel settlements were abandoned, although the evidence here is confused, first by the conversion to
Christianity of their inhabitants and the subsequent change in burial
practice, and second by the similarity of much earlier mid-Saxon pottery
to that which had been used before. Sites at Shepperton and Battersea
continued to be occupied during this period while the exact date of Saxon
occupation at the old Roman settlements of Staines and Brentford is
uncertain. These last two sites probably became important centres for the
administration of their surrounding districts, since one had a reeve and a
minster church while the other was the meeting-place for a church council
(*see* page 66). Both were also documented Saxon river crossings (Edmund's
army crossed the Thames at Brentford in 1016).

From the late seventh century onwards charters survive for many of the
estates in the area, especially a group around Hayes and another group in
north Middlesex. In some cases the boundaries of the estates can be
traced and can be made to agree with medieval parish boundaries for the
same areas, or with logical subdivisions of these boundaries. It is quite
clear that many of these blocks of land were themselves composed of
estates. In the case of Hendon it can be shown that the medieval parish,
which seems to comprise the manor recorded in the Domesday Book, was
three separate estates in the tenth century, one containing Hendon church,
another to the north known as *Lotheresleah* and another, *Blecceanham*,
to the south (*see* Fig. 62). We do not know when this land was divided
up but the way in which boundaries of one estate run on to form the

boundary of the next seems to show that the area was systematically divided, not carved piecemeal out of virgin forest. Neither, so far as can be seen, were the majority of estates formed by the splitting-up of larger entities, although parish names like Great and Little Stanmore suggest that these two parishes were once a single estate. The earliest charters for the clayland are of the late eighth century, which is therefore the latest possible date for the division of the land. In all probability the estates are much earlier than this, but there are two quite separate schools of thought as to just how early. One holds that the estates may actually be of Roman date (some in Middlesex use parts of Watling Street as boundaries) while at the other extreme it is thought that they might have been laid out as part of an attempt to develop the claylands in the seventh century. The opinion of the author is that it is not very likely that detailed boundaries would have survived in the Middlesex or Surrey claylands without a substantial local population passing on the boundaries by 'beating the bounds' or by similar oral transmission. No further development is possible until actual archaeological evidence for the nature of the claylands in the fifth to seventh centuries is produced.

In the absence of substantial archaeological evidence for the later Saxon period the only source of information is the Domesday Book. Surrey, Essex and Middlesex are all included within this survey but London is absent. An estate of the Bishop of London can be identified as a suburb along Bishopsgate, showing that the survey probably only excludes the walled City of London itself. The survey includes a mass of information on tax assessment, land holding and the rural economy and produces a much more detailed picture than archaeology could hope to do. The only problem with using this information is that it tends to colour any inter-pretation of earlier periods and, because its main purpose was to aid tax assessment, land or activities which for one reason or another were not assessed are not mentioned. The information was also collected in different ways in different shires and comparisons of one county with another have to be made with caution.

The following comments are made almost entirely on the basis of a study of the Middlesex Domesday entries, but the entries for that part of Surrey north of the chalk scarp are probably similar. By the late eleventh century the majority of the Thames basin was under the plough. The survey assumes that these ploughs were worked by a team of eight oxen but individual records may well have been converted to 'notional' teams. As part of the assessment, estimates of the total possible ploughland were made and from the difference between these and the actual figures we can see areas which for one reason or another had spare capacity. In Middlesex, Gore Hundred had 30 per cent spare capacity in 1086, whereas Edmonton Hundred apparently had none. Since Edmonton Hundred included areas which were heavily wooded well into the medieval period this does not suggest that the difference between 'land for ploughs' and 'existing ploughs' was an estimate of land that could be assarted. In fact, there is a direct correlation between the decline in value of an estate between 1066 and 1086 and the difference between these two ploughland calculations in the same estates. The 'land for ploughs' figure was therefore probably based on local recollection of what the land could support in the past and an indication that for one reason or another there was less land under the plough in 1086 than twenty years before. Stenton's explanation for this decline in value, which seems plausible, is that it represents the ravaging of the countryside between Berkhamstead and London by William's army in 1066.

The plough oxen would require hay and for this reason meadow land is recorded. In some records surplus hay is noted, which must therefore have been sold. When harvested, the cereal was ground to flour in water-mills. There is a great disparity in the number of mills in different areas and in the value of each mill. At the bottom of the scale is Gore Hundred in north Middlesex which only had one mill, rendering three shillings, while at the other end were areas such as Stepney boasting nine mills rendering in total £10/5s/2d and Staines which had a single mill render-ing sixty four shillings. This disparity would undoubtedly have been reflected in the size and sophistication of the mill itself. At Old Windsor a mill had been constructed by diverting the Thames during the mid or late seventh century, some time later than 668 (Hillam 1981, 42), and it is therefore quite possible that the profitable mills recorded along the Thames in Middlesex and Surrey were on sites originating at this period. When the mill renders are compared with the number of plough teams recorded in the same areas it can be seen that there is a discrepancy. In the Middlesex hundreds, the Kingsbury mill in Gore produced four tenths of a penny per team whilst the average in Elthorne, Spelthorne and Ossulstone was over fifteen pence per team. There could have been considerable regional variation in the use of mills as opposed to hand querns to grind corn (quernstones are common finds in late Saxon London but disappear during the eleventh or early twelfth century), but it is equally likely that grain was being transported between the hundreds to be ground. The high render of the Stepney mills could well have been the result of grain being carted to the outskirts of London before being ground into flour for the use of the citizens. It would have been difficult to build a powerful mill in Gore Hundred because the only source of power available at that time was the headwaters of the river Brent. In the thirteenth century windmills made their first appearance in England, offering an alternative source of power in districts where large rivers were scarce. The Domesday entry for Staines also reveals another benefit of having a mill, since the mill gave a proportion of its render in eels.

Other forms of agriculture were rarely explicitly mentioned in the

Domesday Book but it has been recently suggested that the class of tenant known in Middlesex as a *cotar*, *i.e.* a cottager, is likely to have been employed either in urban occupations (in effect a result of overspill of a borough into the surrounding countryside), or in market gardening since their numbers increase close to towns. All the hundreds in Middlesex had some *cotars* but the highest proportion was to be found in Ossulstone, surrounding the city. The next highest, 23 per cent of named tenants, was to the north of the city in Edmonton Hundred. Analysis of seeds found in tenth and eleventh-century pits in London show that Londoners consumed vast quantities of fruit – apples, cherries and plums in the main – and while it is likely that fruit trees grew within the city these *cotars* are likely to have been responsible for bringing the majority of this fruit into the London markets. Five Domesday estates in Middlesex are recorded as having vineyards, although one is described as newly-planted and therefore a Norman introduction. The majority of the grapes produced were no doubt destined for wine production but grape pips have been found, in small quantities, in the same rubbish deposits described above and in at least one pit from the mid-Saxon Strand settlement.

The Domesday Book is particularly variable when describing livestock. In some counties there appears to have been a realistic head count, at least of those animals on the lord's part of the estate, while in others there is no mention of livestock. Middlesex falls into the latter category. Pasture is mentioned and occasionally it is given a value. Pigs were mentioned, since woodland in Middlesex was estimated by giving a count of the number of pigs that could be supported by it. By and large the Domesday evidence for woodland comes from the same areas as that of place-names which indicate woodland or clearings within woodland. Abundant supplies of wood were present in north Middlesex throughout the medieval period, although there had undoubtedly been much clearance after the Domesday survey. Without detailed fieldwork, excavation, or pollen studies there is little that can be said about the relative percentage of land under wood in the early, mid or late Saxon periods.

The agricultural exploitation of the Thames basin during the Saxon period is crucial for the understanding of London itself but other, smaller, towns also depended on local farming communities for their existence. At present the study of towns other than London has got little further than making lists of which places were towns in the medieval period and hazarding a guess as to when they might have become towns. Excavations at Staines and Brentford have shown that settlement existed there in the Roman period and that there was a centre near Staines, at Binbury, in the mid-Saxon period, but there are no criteria which can be used to say whether the later settlements were urban or not. One would expect that farmers would come to them, pay their taxes at the king's hall, worship at the church and perhaps conduct a bit of business with fellow farmers at the same time (exchanging cows for hens, corn for eels or the like). Whether these settlements actually held tradesmen or artisans is to be doubted. The first evidence for occupation along the High Street at Staines is provided by rubbish pits containing LSS pottery, suggesting that houses fronted the street before *c.* 1050. An eleventh-century town like Uxbridge, on the other hand, would have been much more recognizably urban, although like all medieval market towns it would have been dominated by the buying and selling of rural produce. The results of recent excavation in Uxbridge should produce some evidence to confirm or deny this picture.

The countryside was not just useful to Londoners as a source of provisions or goods for sale. It was also a pleasant place to live. Most Roman cities were surrounded by the villas of the upper classes, those around Verulamium and Cirencester being good examples. London, on the other hand, does not have the same pattern. The only villa within the Thames basin is that at Beddington, which seems more like the dwelling of a farmer with pretensions than the rural residence of a city magnate. In the medieval period there was a steady flow of London merchants into the countryside and from the Domesday Book we know of Londoners, for example canons of St Paul's, who held land outside the city. So far as we know, however, Londoners preferred to relax in the surrounding country-side by hunting. Londoners in the twelfth century claimed rights to hunt in territory as far away as the Chilterns and the estate of *Lotheresleah* was purchased by St Dunstan, sometime Bishop of London, from a hunter in the tenth century.

12 Buildings and daily life

It is an unfortunate feature of the archaeology of Saxon London that on most excavations the ground surface upon which Saxon Londoners lived has been destroyed. The evidence we have for their buildings and the activities which took place within and around them is therefore more limited than it would be, for example, from excavations in York or Lincoln, where large areas of Saxon townscape have survived to be excavated. Nevertheless, if by some miracle we were transported back to Saxon London, archaeology should have prepared us for the appearance of the town and of its inhabitants.

Excavations in the Strand area have produced traces of timber buildings at Jubilee Hall (Blackmore 1986) and The Treasury, Whitehall. These, together with similar evidence from Battersea and Barking, can be used to reconstruct some features of the seventh to ninth-century architecture of the London area. All the buildings discovered to date were built at ground level and were of a rectangular plan. They had walls supported on posts set directly into the ground. Further details must await more discoveries but it is clear that the small sunken-floored buildings which characterise some early Saxon settlements were not ubiquitous in mid-Saxon London. In 1976 these sunken-floored huts were termed Sunken-Featured Buildings or SFBs by Professor Rahtz of the University of York, because it is not known in many cases whether the floors were below ground level or whether the excavated pit actually represents a below-floor cavity. Many were used for weaving. Some of the most common finds in the mid-Saxon Strand settlement are loom weights and indeed the first reconstruction of a Strand mid-Saxon house was made by Sir Mortimer Wheeler, who used a model of a reconstructed hut from Bourton-on-the-Water to show the sort of structure in which the Savoy Palace loom weights might have been used. It is much too soon to say whether he was definitely wrong but at the mid-Saxon *wic* at Southampton there is plentiful evidence for small-scale industry, including weaving, but no SFBs.

There is much more evidence for late Saxon buildings, all from sites within the city walls. This evidence has recently been analysed by a team from the Museum of London (Horsman *et al* 1988). Even when the buildings themselves have not survived it is sometimes possible to show where they were. This was the case at Fish Street Hill, originally the main north-south road from Bishopsgate to London Bridge. As such we can be sure that it was developed as soon as the bridge itself was built. Excavations along the eastern side of the street conducted for the Museum of London by Nick Bateman contrasted with those of his colleague, Gustav Milne, along the western side of Pudding Lane, the next north-south street to the east. At the first site there was a strip of land devoid of Saxon features, while further back from the road, and at the same height, there were numerous pits and traces of two successive buildings with sunken floors. At Pudding Lane, by contrast, the land alongside the lane was peppered with pits of tenth-century date over which were traces of ground-level buildings. These buildings utilised terraces constructed in the Roman period. The earliest of these buildings dated to the end of the tenth or beginning of the eleventh century. At Botolph Lane, three small areas were dug by Milne to the east of the lane. He and his team also dug a section across the lane, the line of which was regrettably later destroyed by the redevelopment. They were able to show that there may have been activity on the site after the deposition of 'dark earth' during or after the late Roman period but that the site had been laid out afresh in the late ninth or tenth century. A dump of earth underlay the earliest buildings fronting onto Botolph Lane and what appears to be the same dump underlay the lane itself. Here too, therefore, the street frontage dates from the beginning of the late Saxon reoccupation of this part of the city.

Similar evidence was recovered from Well Court, Bow Lane, although there it was possible that there might have been a period of time after the construction of Bow Lane before the laying-out of the first timber building fronting the lane (*see* Fig. 11). The excavation area was too small to be certain about this and would in any case not prove that buildings were not lining the street elsewhere.

Excavations at Milk Street, a side street to the north of Cheapside, produced similar evidence to Fish Street Hill. The earliest Saxon building found there dated to the late ninth to early eleventh century but only fragmentary remains of the floors of ground-level timber buildings were found. They were fronting onto Milk Street and were constructed during the late tenth or early eleventh century. These remains formed the back wall and floors of two successive ground-level buildings running parallel with the line of Milk Street. Later, a pit was cut through the floor of these buildings. This pit was one of a number running at right angles to the street which form further evidence that the street existed by the early eleventh century. Further away from the streets the pits became more numerous. It is likely that this area was less intensively occupied than Fish Street Hill, so that initially buildings could be set along the street instead of perpendicular to it. Further evidence for ground-level buildings along the street frontages was found in excavations at Watling Court, a large site bounded by Basing Lane (now replaced by Cannon Street) on the south and Bow Lane on the east. Here too the buildings themselves did not survive but there were unpitted areas along both frontages. The fact that these pits included cess pits dated to the late ninth to early eleventh centuries suggests that there were buildings on the street frontages by then.

A fourth small excavation at Ironmonger Lane produced the remains of two very crude sunken-featured buildings of late ninth to early eleventh-

FIG. 69   A sunken-featured building from Ironmonger Lane, London. Looking west, with a one-metre scale. (Museum of London)

century date (*see* Fig. 69). These were abandoned, filled in and a ground-level timber building erected over the top during the early eleventh century. The site then appeared to have been disused for some time and the first definite evidence for further use of the site can be dated to the late eleventh or early twelfth century, by which time it seems that Ironmonger Lane certainly existed with timber buildings erected at the frontage.

These excavations, and several others, seem to show that there were some streets in the city which were laid out and occupied from the beginning of the reoccupation of the city, whilst there were others, like Pudding Lane and Ironmonger Lane, which either did not exist or were not built up until a later date. However, by no means all buildings in late Saxon London were ranged along the street frontages. Several excavations have produced traces of sunken-floored buildings, and by this late Saxon date there is no difficulty in saying that it is the floors themselves which are sunken. Such buildings were always set back from the street frontage; indeed it is likely that they were mostly ranged along the back or sides of the properties. Usually the surface from which they were constructed has gone, but it is quite clear that they varied considerably in depth as well as in construction techniques and sophistication. Some of the shallowest were at Milk Street and Ironmonger Lane. At Milk Street traces of wooden steps were found, showing that one entered the building from the east rather than through the backyard of buildings fronting onto Milk Street (*see* Fig. 70). Buildings behind the Fish Street Hill frontage and at Pudding Lane had similar shallow 'cellars' and the majority of the building must have stood above ground level. However, when the Pudding Lane building was backfilled it could be seen that the backfill contained large fragments of a pond deposit through which the building had been cut. Valerie Horsman of the Museum of London concluded from this that the upcast from the building's floor had been piled up around the walls, to form a low bank of earth (Horsman *et al* 1988, 100–101 and Fig. 98). Much deeper structures were found on the Watling Court site. They would have been deep enough to form completely subterranean cellars – the largest was 2.3 metres deep – and were considerably bigger that those previously mentioned.

Very soon after the Norman conquest there is evidence for the building of stone-cellared buildings, at Milk Street for example. Secular stone buildings may have been used in Saxon London too but the only pre-conquest mortared foundations discovered to date, from Pudding Lane and Fish Street Hill, probably supported timber baseplates. In Asser's *Life of King Alfred* we are specifically told that the king constructed royal halls and chambers in stone and that royal residences in stone were 'moved at the royal command from their ancient sites and beautifully erected in more suitable places' (Whitelock 1968, No. 7 Ch. 91, 272). The presumed purpose of moving stone houses would be to place them

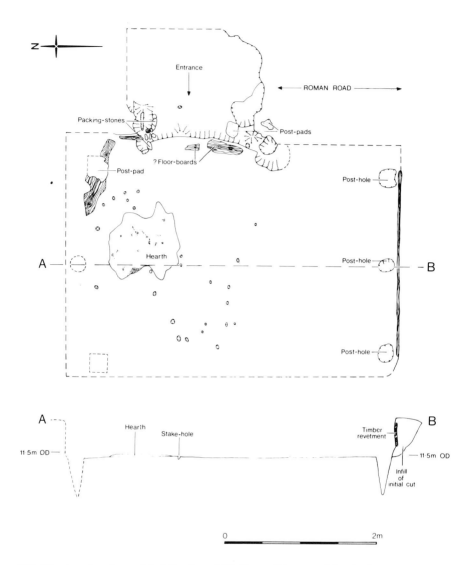

FIG. 70   A sunken-featured building from Milk Street. (Museum of London)

inside *burhs* and it seems quite possible that this happened at London.

Our knowledge of house interiors is slight, since we can only comment upon ground floors and cellars. Buildings with upper storeys existed and are known from documentary sources. For example, one at Calne in Wiltshire collapsed, bringing about the death of some of the English council (Whitelock 1968, No. 1, 210). Nevertheless, buildings with two above-ground stories are thought to have been restricted to the upper classes. Some of the deeper sunken-floored buildings from London produced no evidence for a hearth and were presumably cellars used for storage below a ground-level hall.

Excavated floors consisted of clay or brickearth and on top of these were spreads of black 'occupation debris'. Samples of these deposits have been examined by palaeobotanists who have shown that they contain high quantities of rush seeds. They must therefore represent the remains of a spread of rushes overlying the earth floor. When this surface was soiled it could be swept up and discarded in a rubbish pit or midden, taking with it small artefacts which had been dropped or thrown away onto the floor. Two buildings at Pudding Lane had smashed fragments of large pottery spouted storage jars on their floors, showing that these vessels were used in the house. Small pottery lamps provided lighting. In the tenth and early eleventh centuries these lamps were provided with pedestals or splayed bases and must have sat on the floor or on a niche in the wall. In the later eleventh century they were provided with spikes and lips. This form was copying the common glass form, used for centuries within the Church, which is often shown in manuscripts as being suspended from the vault (*see* Fig. 71).

Late Saxon buildings were normally provided with a central hearth, usually consisting of baked clay overlying a bed of stone to retain the heat. Pottery cooking pots show that the fires were allowed to die down before the pots were set in the embers. Quite often the pot fragments are caked with burnt food or with scale which accumulated through the use

FIG. 71 A tenth or eleventh-century pottery lamp from the city of London. (Museum of London)

of the pot to boil water. More open pottery forms were used for cooking as well. They were usually provided with handles and may have been used like modern saucepans and frying pans. It is now possible to identify the residues of food cooked in pottery vessels but we do not know whether a meat and vegetable sauce would produce a different chemical signature to a 'fry-up'. We have no evidence that metal vessels were in common use in Saxon London although there is plentiful evidence in Anglo-Saxon literature for the use of the large metal cauldron. Their absence from excavations in London may be due to the fact that copper alloy vessels could be melted down and reused, but they would certainly have been much more valuable than pottery. Wooden vessels would have been quite common but only survive in exceptional circumstances since they could be thrown onto the fire if broken. Fragments of a large bread-making trough and a wooden ladle have been found, together with bowls and waste, which shows that they were being made in London using a pole lathe.

Much is made of drinking in Anglo-Saxon literature. Wine was probably one of the imports into mid-Saxon London, as is suggested by the sherds of imported pitchers from the Strand (*see* Fig. 72). Late tenth and eleventh-century imported pottery is also likely to have entered London alongside wine and was used both to serve and to drink it (*see* Fig. 73). The distribution of pitchers and beakers in refuse pits suggests that much drinking took place in the home, as well as communally. Water was supplied by wells and a few have been found in excavations, both in the Strand settlement and in the walled city. A late eleventh-century example from Watling Court was lined with reused wine barrels (*see* Fig. 74), and the same technique may have been used in the mid-Saxon town, since an undated well constructed of silver-fir wine barrels was recently found on an excavation close to Trafalgar Square.

Clothing in Saxon times was made of woollen cloth, linen and some silk (*see* Fig. 48); of these, woollen cloth was by far the most important. Most evidence for the appearance of clothing comes from contemporary illustrations, mainly accompanying religious works and not therefore representative of what town-dwellers might wear. Scraps of cloth have survived in rubbish pits at Milk Street and Watling Court and these show that high-quality fabrics were available in tenth and eleventh-century London (Pritchard 1984). The silk would have been used for garters, edging and hair nets, the sort of use which would show off the material to greatest effect. Metal pins, either of copper alloy or silver, were used in the early and mid-Saxon periods to fasten clothes but later become rare. In their place, perhaps, large bone pins which sometimes have crudely-decorated heads were used. Some of these were decorated in 'Ringerike' style, which first appeared in London in the early to mid-eleventh century. Belts and straps were used throughout the Saxon period and buckles and strap-ends were often elaborately decorated (*see* Fig. 75). The narrow

FIG. 72   A mid-Saxon imported pitcher, probably made in northern France in the seventh century. From the excavation at Maiden Lane, London, carried out by the Museum of London. (Museum of London)

FIG. 73   A Rhenish red-painted ware beaker from London. (Museum of London)

FIG. 74 A wattle-lined pit at Watling Court, London. (Museum of London)

strap-end was particularly common in the mid-Saxon period and examples are known from the Strand settlement. A few loose examples are known from within the city walls but unfortunately none come from recent excavations. Later Saxon belts were usually wider and their buckles were often decorated with animal and foliage patterns similar to the Winchester style, used in the decorative arts and which flourished in the late tenth and early eleventh centuries. The earliest leather shoes known from Saxon London date to the tenth or early eleventh centuries. All the examples known were made in simple utilitarian styles and were sewn together with leather thongs. Groups of mid-eleventh-century shoes show the use of thread (either flax or wool) and have some purely decorative elements, such as thonging. Late eleventh-century shoes show continued use of decoration, including vamp stripes made with silk and exaggeration to the toe. Such fashions were recorded at the court of William II but it is revealing to see that they were being followed in London.

Much of our information about daily life in Saxon London comes from the filling of rubbish pits. Most excavations in both the mid-Saxon and late Saxon towns have been peppered with pits, often a metre or so in diameter and between one and three metres deep (*see* Fig. 76). Many were originally used as latrines and the surrounding subsoil has been stained green through the action of the cess. (Strictly speaking this is probably due to the reduction of iron compounds caused by the anaerobic

FIG. 75 Saxon jewellery from London. Part of the hoard of late tenth or eleventh-century pewter found at Cheapside. (Museum of London)

FIG. 76 Rubbish pits at Watling Court. (Museum of London)

conditions such pits created.) At Watling Court each layer within a pit was isolated and excavated separately. Study of the finds and soil samples from these pits shows that layers of cess often alternated with tips of garden soil, domestic refuse and floor sweepings. Amongst the less savoury items preserved in rubbish pits are dog coprolites (de Rouffignac 1985, 105). Their high bone content shows that dogs were scavengers in mid-Saxon London and in late Saxon Southwark, although no such finds have yet been reported from late Saxon London. Other pits were used solely as cess pits and have a thick layer of cess at the base followed by a capping layer of soil. There are traces of plank and wattle linings on eleventh century pits but not in earlier ones. This suggests that by the eleventh century the pit contents may have been periodically cleared out, as was normal in the later medieval period. If true, this may have been because the city was becoming more intensively occupied or because the night soil was being used as manure on the city fields.

Both archaeologists and the general public often ask about the racial composition of Londoners in the Saxon period. Between the late fourth and the eleventh centuries at least four major groups are known to have lived in London: the British, the Anglo-Saxons, the Scandinavians and the Norman French. Each group was distinguished by language and customs. However, archaeology is a very blunt instrument to use when studying race since it emphasises the similarities between people who themselves thought they had a very distinct identity. The main evidence for the survival of Britons in the London area comes from place-names. The names for some natural features derive from Celtic or Latin names. Bedfont, near Staines, for example is thought to include the Latin word for spring, *fons*, while the river Brent appears to have been named after the Celtic word for 'high or holy river', *Brigantia* (Ekwall 1960, 34 and 63). By and large, however, the names of settlements and landscape features in the London area are Anglo-Saxon even when, as at Walworth or Walbrook, they may record the presence of the Welsh. In the Anglo-Saxon language, however, there was no difference between the word for Welsh and that for slave.

In the Danelaw many place-names are wholly or partly Scandinavian in origin and testify to a substantial influx of Scandinavian-speakers in some areas. In the London area such evidence is almost entirely lacking. Gunnersbury, in west London, is named after a lady with a Scandinavian name and probably dates to the period after Cnut's conquest in 1016, when Danes obtained a privileged position in society. A runic inscription on a richly-carved tombstone, found to the south of St Paul's Cathedral, shows that it was erected for and by Danes. A fragment of a similar Scandinavian style grave-marker from All Hallows Barking is probably contemporary but is not inscribed. The names of moneyers recorded on their coins, the names of church founders surviving in the church name and the few individual Londoners' names which were recorded in documents all show that within the upper levels of London society from the early eleventh century onwards Scandinavians formed a substantial minority. Scandinavian influence on decoration also became more and more common but this does not mean that a substantial element of London's population was Scandinavian, only that Scandinavian taste was fashionable. Throughout the post-conquest medieval period, the royal court led changes in fashion and this must have also been the case in the late Saxon period. The influence of the early Norman royal court on shoe fashion has already been mentioned but in many respects the Norman influence on material culture in London was surprisingly small, or at least so gradual that it is impossible to say that any development took place as a result of the conquest.

Apart from these four groups, other nationalities are recorded in London during the Saxon period, such as a Frisian slave-trader in the seventh century or German clerics at St Martin-le-Grand in the eleventh century. They show that London would have always been frequented by foreigners so long as there was foreign trade. Ethelred's law code not only lists the origin of some of these merchants but also shows that the presence of all but the Danes was controlled. Finds such as brooches which are almost certainly of German or Frisian origin may have entered London as the personal belongings of a trader or his entourage, or may have been sold in the city as trinkets. It is probably impossible to tell which.

Probably the most reliable way to determine the composition of the population is by the study of excavated skeletons. Two groups of late Saxon burials from London have been examined: those from St Nicholas Shambles and the church which preceded Holy Trinity Priory. Both are very late, probably starting in the middle of the eleventh century and both contain burials of post-conquest date, although those from Holy Trinity Priory are earlier than *c.* 1100. From these studies we learn that men probably outnumbered women in London but that women and children were certainly present. One sad find records the death of a woman and her baby during labour before childbirth. We learn that late Saxon and early Norman Londoners differed little from the average in stature, that their diet lead to their having less tooth decay than we have now but much greater tooth wear. We learn of injuries and disease and that life expectancy was closer to forty years than seventy (White 1988, 29–50). Studies of occupation and cess deposits show that parasitic worms – maw worm, tapeworm, and whip-worm – were endemic and that a low standard of hygiene was maintained (de Rouffignac 1985, 105; 1989). Through the study of abnormalities in bone structure, we learn that families were often buried close together within graveyards, but not definitely in family plots.

Conclusion

One danger in writing about Saxon London is that the reader is led to believe that the place was special. First, London is big and complex enough to give writers little space to mention other towns or areas. Archaeologists can spend their whole working lives in London and simply not know how their evidence compares with that found elsewhere. Second, when one writes that London was bigger or earlier or distinguished from other towns this is greeted with scepticism by other archaeologists, who think they recognise public relations 'hype'. So, how far is it justified to treat London as an exception, and how typical is London of Saxon towns in general?

Throughout this book I have compared and contrasted late Roman London and Verulamium. There is little doubt in my mind that the two towns suffered different fates. In several Romano-British towns the end of occupation seems to have come suddenly, but not violently, and to have been preceded by a change in use of the walled area. The forum at Gloucester was demolished during the late fourth century and a metalled area laid over its site before 400. At Lincoln some stone buildings were abandoned during the third quarter of the fourth century, although occupation must have continued somewhere in the town to account for the spread of late fourth-century pottery and coins. These towns therefore suffered a similar fate to London even though both were within areas where a late survival of British independence is likely. The conclusion which must be drawn from this is that round about 400 there was a major disruption to the economy in Britain, as a result of which towns, villas, industries and coinage vanished from the province. It is worth emphasising that this collapse does not seem to be the consequence of Germanic settlement, which began on a large scale a generation later.

Some sort of British presence within the walls of late Roman towns in the fifth century is demonstrated not only at Wroxeter and Verulamium but also at Silchester and Canterbury. In the latter cases, however, there is no indication that this presence was urban. They are more likely to have formed aristocratic or ecclesiastical centres, possibly within a much shrunken core. Such evidence may one day come from London but cannot alter the general picture of decay and abandonment.

There is no doubt from the evidence amassed to date that London was eventually completely deserted, both within the walls and along the Strand, although it is still just possible that a substantial early Saxon settlement awaits discovery on yet another site in the London area. The rebirth of London took place in the seventh century, if not in the late sixth century, and can be compared with evidence from *Hamwic*, Canterbury, Ipswich, and York. Excavations at these towns have shown that all were in existence by the end of the seventh century. *Hamwic* certainly seems to have started later than London and Ipswich while Canterbury, which has produced evidence for sixth-century occupation within its walls, is almost certainly earlier. The York evidence has yet to be evaluated but the existence of a mint by the 640s can be postulated (Stewart 1978, 149). London therefore appears to stand naturally in the middle of a sequence of towns, starting in Kent, spreading up the east coast of England and eventually spreading along the south coast. This evidence fits well with current ideas about the use of coins in seventh-century England.

The seventh-century town at London appears to have been relatively small, as does that at Ipswich, but the eighth and ninth-century settlement was much bigger. The only way in which we can compare sizes at this period is from the archaeological evidence and many assumptions have to be made: whether settlement was continuous or seasonal, for example. Nevertheless, the density of pit-digging found on a Strand settlement excavation compares well with the density found at *Hamwic* or Ipswich and it therefore seems reasonable to assume that a greater extent of occupation evidence is due to a larger population. On this basis, London seems to have been twice as big as Ipswich and *Hamwic*, both of which cover just over forty hectares.

We have very little information at present about the internal organisation of the Strand settlement. Traces of rectangular timber buildings — rubbish pits, wells, metalled surfaces and a timber waterfront — have been found but we cannot yet make sensible comparisons between one part of the settlement and another, or between the different stages in the development of the town. The *Hamwic* settlement at St Mary's, Southampton, was not subsequently so heavily built up as the Strand and excavations there have been able to show that the town was laid out on a regular grid. Wide, metalled roads were constructed before settlement began and a small ditch marked out the boundary of the settlement. These features, together with the orderly nature of the buildings which lined the streets, contrast with the sprawling, irregular plan to be found on contemporary rural settlements. They must imply a centralised control of the foundation of *Hamwic*. By the late seventh century *Lundenwic* too is likely to have been under direct royal control. What archaeology will soon be able to tell us is whether this is also true for the early seventh-century or earlier town.

The archaeological evidence for the abandonment of the Strand settlement must be compared with that from the other *wic* sites in England and the Continent. Pottery cannot be dated precisely for this period and there is no relevant dendrochronological evidence. However, coins have been found on all these sites and they indicate a drop in coin-loss starting in the early ninth century. This evidence has been used to show that the *wics* were in decline before the Viking invasions started in the 860s. There is no reason to doubt the truth of this. It would say something extraordinary about the strength of the ninth-century economy of England if the level of raiding to which it must have been subjected had no effect on the volume of trade. This coin evidence should not be pushed too far, however, and in the Thames valley there are several coin hoards of the 860s and early in the 870s which show that a mixed coinage was circulating, including pieces from East Anglia, Wessex and both the Carolingian and Arab worlds. These hoards are not different in character from the Middle Temple hoard of the 840s. Soon after, however, coin production came to an almost complete standstill.

East Anglia was once a major trading partner of London's, as demonstrated by the frequency with which East Anglian coins and pots are found in the London area. In 868 the East Anglian kingdom fell to the Vikings and the coins issued by the new Viking rulers are rarely found outside the Danelaw. Not only are Viking coins extremely rare in the London area but those coins which circulated in the Danelaw were often scratched with the point of a knife, to check their purity, but no London examples are known of these 'pecked' coins which could have circulated in the Danelaw and then returned to Wessex (of which London was now a part). The coinage used in and around London in this period is almost entirely English (Stott 1989). Late ninth and early tenth-century evidence from the Danelaw shows that there was, by contrast, considerable contact between the new Viking states – York, the five boroughs, East Anglia and Dublin – together with some evidence for contact with the Viking homeland. In the eighth century London was the only port which the Mercian kings controlled directly, rather than through a client king, so that their trading contacts with East Anglia, Kent and the Continent were carried out through London. By the end of the ninth century, by contrast, London was marginalised.

The evidence from London does, however, compare well with other English towns outside of the Danelaw. By the end of the ninth century, most of these towns were probably defended but there is little archaeological evidence to show that they initially contained large populations. York and Lincoln, on the other hand, had side streets lined with buildings by the beginning of the tenth century. We know from documentary evidence that the English *burhs* were sometimes provided with markets and a street system as well as defences from the start. The Queenhithe charters for London can be compared with another grant held by Worcester Cathedral which confirms that Worcester itself was provided with fortifications, a market and streets by 899 (Whitelock 1968, No. 99, 498). That Worcester contained, or was at least intended to contain, a permanent population is indicated by a reference to land-rent. Notwithstanding these intentions, the archaeological evidence from Worcester as well as from towns such as Gloucester and Bath suggests that it was only during the tenth century that the English *burhs* actually started to grow. There is too little precision in archaeological dating for this period to chart this growth in detail, either in London or elsewhere in England outside the Danelaw.

From the end of the tenth century onwards the archaeological evidence from London becomes much more informative. This is both due to the rapidity with which pottery types were changing at this time and also to the major changes which were taking place along the waterfront. Together, these circumstances allow us to reconstruct the development of the water-front. The absence of finds or structures earlier than the late tenth century on any waterfront site excavated to date is remarkable and suggests that until the end of the century the riverside wall acted as a barrier and that only a small number of quays existed, possibly even just one, at Queen-hithe. Late in the tenth century the first signs of activity along the waterfront have been found at New Fresh Wharf and are possibly con-nected with the construction of back lanes, such as Pudding Lane, leading down to the river from the market square at Eastcheap. In the middle of the eleventh century this small-scale use of the waterfront expanded rapidly so that by *c.* 1050 there was probably an almost continuous artificial bank running in front of the wall in the eastern half of the city. At the same time the quantity of imported pottery used in the city rose. This change can be seen not just amongst material deposited along the waterfront but throughout the city. The apparent size of the tenth-century settlement, the evidence of Athelstan's laws concerning moneyers and the size of the Danegeld paid by the citizens of London following Cnut's conquest all show that London before the middle of the eleventh century was already a place of considerable importance, but from our archae-ological evidence it is certainly not clear that this importance was based on trade between England and the Danelaw or the Continent.

Both the English *burhs* and the Danish boroughs were provided in the late ninth and early tenth centuries with defences of differing length. This length was itself related to the garrison needed to man them. In time, the available space within the fortifications outgrew that provided by the founders and settlement spread outside the walls into undefended suburbs. The position of Southwark is unclear in this context. Although its name shows that it was defended and it appears in the *Burghal Hidage* with 1,800 hides, which would allow a wall 2,263 metres long to be manned, there is no archaeological evidence for its defences. The only evidence for settlement there in the tenth or early eleventh centuries comes from the extreme northern end of the later town. In all probability, the settlement existed as a defended bridgehead only, until Borough High Street was laid out with St George's church at its southern end. Rubbish pits show that by the late eleventh to early twelfth centuries there was occupation all along the High Street. Other towns have produced similar evidence for the development of suburbs within the late Saxon period, but it seems that London suburbs may be slightly later than most. If so, this is probably because of the large size of the initial defended area. Similarly, the proliferation of late Saxon churches is found in many towns but London seems to have more of a mid-eleventh-century date than most other towns, although the London sample is quite likely to be biased towards the smallest churches, many of which went out of use at the time of the Great Fire or before.

To answer the questions posed as the beginning of this chapter, it does seem that London developed in the Saxon period along a path trodden by only a handful of other English towns. All were situated on navigable rivers on the east or south coast and in at least three cases – Southampton, Canterbury and York – the Anglo-Saxon town was situated close to a walled Roman town which seems to have been kept clear of settlement until the late ninth century. At that time the foundation of the *burhs* by the West Saxon kings and of similar fortifications by the Vikings gave an impetus to urban development. In the Danelaw populous towns were again in existence by *c.* 900, but in Wessex and Mercia, including London, the *burhs* may have remained sparsely populated fortresses until well into the tenth century.

The growth of London in the later tenth and eleventh centuries is shared to some extent by almost all towns in England inside and outside the Danelaw, where excavation has taken place. Despite the evidence for the rapid growth of international trade in the middle of the eleventh century, it is moreover probably the increasing interest of the king in London (itself perhaps a reflection of the growing wealth of the community) which set the scene for London's later predominance.

To conclude, if one thing is certain about Anglo-Saxon archaeology, and indeed about all archaeology in London, it is that it is impossible to predict what will turn up next. Any attempt to do so would probably be laughably wrong. Nevertheless, there are some areas where we already know that there is data but that data has not yet been analysed. Within the next decade we should have considerably more information about Saxon animal husbandry and the organisation of the meat trade. It has been suggested at other sites that mid-Saxon livestock was larger than that of the late Saxon and early medieval periods. We now have the data to tell whether this is true of London. If so, it would be a further indication of the disruption caused by the Viking invasions. We should also know more about the settlement density around London, but perhaps only if we make a special effort to recover the data. It would be extremely easy to decide that Greater London was not the best place to study Saxon rural settlement, but it is only close to London that the effect, if any, of the growth of London on the countryside will be seen.

Finally, there are specific points which need to be clarified and which could be sorted out if the right sites were found. First, a tighter chronology for late ninth to eleventh-century London is required. Any clarification of the chronology of this period will help the historical interpretation of the archaeological results and would have an effect throughout the Thames valley as far west as Oxford.

Second, we need more evidence for the relative date of the Cheapside and Eastcheap street grids. We are fairly certain that Cheapside was in existence at the time of the Queenhithe charters but the evidence from the eastern part of the city is much less certain. Providing a date for the Eastcheap grid would also help to date the rebuilding of London Bridge and define the strategic importance of Southwark more closely. It may well be that analysis of the timbers recently found at the Southwark end of London Bridge will provide an answer.

Third, there is virtually no archaeological evidence for land-use within the city walls in the mid-Saxon period. So far, the only actual archaeological deposit which dates between the seventh and the late ninth centuries to be found within the walls of London is a freshwater marsh. Particular care should be taken in the future to find and analyse evidence of this period within the walls. When, for example, was the name Cornhill appropriate for the eastern hill of London?

Last, we must have more evidence for the date and character of the desertion of the Strand settlement. The earliest areas of late Saxon settlement were at either ends of the settlement and were suburbs which grew up outside the walled city and Westminster. There, if anywhere, evidence for continuous occupation from the mid-ninth century to the eleventh century might be found. By the 870s the Strand settlement may have shrunk to nothing, although the numismatic evidence suggests that it would have still been an active settlement at the time of the Viking invasion of Mercia. Excavations at *Hamwic* have shown that it was still occupied into the reign of Alfred and both there and in London the transition between the old trading centre and the embryo medieval town is unclear.

Bibliography

I have not given a reference for every statement in this book, especially not in Part One, and those wishing to follow up any unattributed statements made here should start with the bibliographies provided in Biddle (1976), Dyson and Schofield (1984), Hobley (1985; 1988) and Vince (1989). New discoveries are usually mentioned in *The London Archaeologist* and fully published in the *Transactions of the London and Middlesex Archaeological Society* or in their Special Papers series. Recent statements on the archaeological evidence from *Hamwic*, Ipswich and York can be found in Hodges and Hobley (1988).

ALCOCK, L.: *Dinas Powys: An Iron Age, Dark Age and Early Medieval Settlement in Glamorgan*, University of Wales Press, 1963.

ALCOCK, L.: '*By South Cadbury is that Camelot...*': *Excavations at Cadbury Castle 1966–70*, Thames and Hudson, 1972.

ARCHIBALD, M.: 'Anglo-Saxon and Norman lead objects with official coin types', in Vince, A. (ed.) *Aspects of Saxo-Norman London II: Finds and Environmental evidence*, LAMAS Special Paper 12, 1989.

ARTHUR, P. and WHITEHOUSE, K.: 'Report on excavations at Fulham Palace Moat, 1972–1973', in *Trans LAMAS*, 29, 1978, 45–72.

BAILEY, K.: 'The Middle Saxons', in Bassett, S. (ed.) *The Origins of the Anglo-Saxon Kingdoms*, Leicester Univ Press, 1989.

BARTHOLOMEW, P.: 'Fourth-Century Saxons', in *Britannia* XV, 1984, 169–186.

BASCOMBE, K.: 'Two charters of King Suabred of Essex', in Neale, K. (ed.) *An Essex Tribute to S. F. Emerson*, 1987, 85–96.

BENDER-JORGENSEN, L.: 'Prehistoric Scandinavian Textiles', in *Nordiske Fortydsminder* Serie B bind 9, Copenhaven, 1986.

BIDDLE, M.: 'Excavations at Winchester, 1971. Tenth and final interim report: Part I', in *Antiquaries Journal*, 55, 1975, 96–126.

BIDDLE, M.: 'Winchester in the early middle ages', in *Winchester Studies* 1, Oxford University Press, 1976.

BIDDLE, M.: 'Towns', in Wilson, D. (ed.) *The Archaeology of Anglo-Saxon England*, Methuen, 1976, 99–150.

BIDDLE, M. and HILL, D.: 'Late Saxon Planned Towns', in *Antiquaries Journal* 51, 1971, 70–85.

BIDDLE, M.: 'London on the Strand', in *Popular Archaeology* July 1984, 23–7.

BLACKMORE, L.: 'Des. res. (close City and Thames): Early and middle Saxon buildings in the Greater London area', in *The London Archaeologist* 5 No. 8, Autumn 1986, 207–16.

BLAIR, J.: 'Frithuwald's kingdom and the origins of Surrey', in Bassett, S. (ed.) *The Origins of the Anglo-Saxon Kingdoms*, Leicester University Press, 1989.

BLUNT, C. E., LYON, C. S. S. and STEWART, I.: 'The coinage of southern England, 796–840', in *British Numismatic Journal* 32, 1964, 1–64.

BORIUS, R.: 'Vie de Saint Germain d'Auxerre', in *Sources Chretiennes* 112, 1965.

BROOKE, C. and KEIR, G.: *London 800–1216: The Shaping of a City*, Secker and Warburg, 1975.

CASTLE, S.: 'Excavations in Pear Wood, Brockley Hill, Middlesex, 1948–1973', in *Trans LAMAS* 26, 1975, 267–77.

CHAPLIN, R. E.: *The study of Animal Bones from Archaeological Sites*, Seminar Press, 1971.

COWIE, R.: 'Lundenwic: Unravelling the Strand', in *Archaeology Today* 8 No. 5, 1987 30–34.

CUNLIFFE, B. W.: *The Temple of Sulis Minerva at Bath 1(ii) The site*, OUCA, 1985.

DAVIS, A. and DE MOULINS, D.: 'Plant remains from Maiden Lane and Jubilee Hall', forthcoming.

DAVIS, R. H. C.: 'Alfred and Guthrum's Frontier', in *English Historical Review* XCVII, 1982, 803–10.

DAVIS, R. H. C.: 'The Carmen de Hastingae Proelio', in *English Historical Review* 93, 1978, 241–61.

DENSEM, R. and SEALEY, D.: 'Excavations at Rectory Grove, Clapham, 1980–1', in *The London Archaeologist* 4 No. 7, 177–84.

DE ROUFFIGNAC, C.: 'Parasite egg survival and indentification from Hibernia Wharf, Southwark', in *The London Archaeologist* 5 No. 4, 1985, 103–5.

DYSON, T.: 'Two Saxon land grants at Queenhithe', in Bird, J., Chapman, H. and Clark, J. (eds.) *Collectanea Londiniensia: studies ... presented to R Merrifield*, LAMAS Special Paper 2, 1978, 200–215.

DYSON, T.: 'London and Southwark in the Seventh Century and later: a neglected reference', in *Trans LAMAS* 31, 1980, 83–95.

DYSON, T. and SCHOFIELD, J.: 'Excavations in the City of London: Second Interim Report, 1974–1978', in *Trans LAMAS* 32, 1981, 24–81.

DYSON, T. and SCHOFIELD, J.: 'Saxon London', in Haslam, J. *Anglo-Saxon Towns*, Phillimore, 1984, 285–313.

EKWALL, E.: *The Concise Oxford Dictionary of English Place-names*, Clarendon Press, Oxford, 4th Edition 1960.

EVISON, V.: 'The Saxon Objects', in Hurst, J. G. 'The kitchen area of Northolt Manor, Middlesex', in *Medieval Archaeology* 5, 1961, 211–299.

FRERE, S.: *Verulamium Excavations* II, Reports of the Research Committee of the Society of Antiquaries of London XVI, 1983.

GELLING, M.: *The Early Charters of the Thames Valley*, Leicester University Press, 1979.

GEM, R.: 'Chapter One: The origins of the Abbey', in Wilson, C. *Westminster Abbey*, 1986.

GIBBS, M.: *Early Charters of the Cathedral Church of St Paul, London*, Camden Third Series LVIII, 1939.

GOING, C.: 'A Middle Saxon buckle from Lincoln Road, Enfield', in *The London Archaeologist* 5 No. 11, 301–2.

GRIERSON, P. and BLACKBURN, M.: *Medieval European coinage; 1 the early Middle Ages (5th–10th centuries)*, Cambridge University Press, 1986.

GRIMES, W. F.: *The Archaeology of Roman and Medieval London*, London, 1968.

GRIMES, W. F.: 'Introduction: The Archaeological Background', in Toynbee, J. M. C. *The Roman Art Treasures from the Temple of Mithras*, LAMAS Special Paper 7, 1986.

HALL, R.: *The Viking Dig: The Excavations at York*, Bodley Head, 1984.

HALL, R.: 'York 700−1050', in Hodges, R. and Hobley, B. (eds.) *The Rebirth of Towns in the West AD 700−1050*, CBA Research Report 68, 1988, 125−132.

HARDEN, D. B.: 'Glass Vessels in Britain and Ireland AD 400−1000', in Harden, D. B. (ed.) *Dark Age Britain*, Methuen, 1956, 132−70.

HASLAM, J.: 'The excavation of a section across Aldersgate Street, City of London, 1972', in *Trans LAMAS* 24, 1973, 74−84.

HASLAM, J.: 'The Towns of Wiltshire', in Haslam, J. *Anglo-Saxon Towns*, Phillimore, 1984, 87−147.

HASLAM, J.: 'The Metrology of Anglo-Saxon Cricklade', in *Medieval Archaeology* XXX, 1986, 99−103.

HASLAM, J.: 'Parishes, Churches, Wards and Gates in Eastern London', in Blair, J. (ed.) in *Minster and Parish Churches: The Local Church in Transition 950−1200*, Oxford University Committee for Archaeology, 1988, 35−43.

HAWKES, S. C. and DUNNING, G. C.: 'Soldiers and settlers in Britain, fourth to fifth century: with a catalogue of animal-ornamented buckles and related belt-fittings', in *Medieval Archaeology* V, 1961, 1−70.

HEIGHWAY, C. M.: **'Excavations at Gloucester: fourth interim report', in** *Antiquaries Jnl* 58, 1978, 125−8.

HILL, C. et al: *The Roman Riverside Wall and Monumental Arch in London*, LAMAS Special Paper 3, 1980.

HILL, D.: 'The Burghal Hidage: The Establishment of a Text', in *Medieval Archaeology*, 13, 1969, 84−92.

HILL, D.: 'London Bridge: a reasonable doubt?', in *Trans LAMAS* 27, 1976, 303−4.

HILLAM, J.: 'An English Tree-Ring Chronology, AD 404−1216', in *Medieval Archaeology* XXV, 1981, 31−44.

HOBLEY, B.: 'Saxon London: Lundenwic and Lundenburh, two cities rediscovered', in Hodges, R. and Hobley, B. (eds.) 1988, 69−82.

HODGES, R.: *The Hamwih pottery*, CBA Research Report 37, 1981.

HODGES, R.: *Dark Age economics*, Duckworth, 1982.

HODGES, R. and HOBLEY, B. (eds.): *The Rebirth of Towns in the West AD 700−1050*, CBA Research Report 68, 1988.

HORSMAN, V., MILNE, C. and MILNE, G.: *Aspects of Saxo-Norman London I*, LAMAS Special Paper 11, 1988.

HUGGINS, P. J.: 'Excavations of Belgic and Romano-British Farm with Middle Saxon Cemetery and Churches at Nazeingbury, Essex, 1975−6', in *Essex Archaeology and History* 10, 1978, 29−117.

HURST, J. G.: 'The kitchen area of Northolt Manor, Middlesex', in *Medieval Archaeology* 5, 1961, 211−299.

JOHNSON, T.: 'A Roman Signal Tower at Shadwell, E.1 − an interim note', in *Trans LAMAS* 26, 1975, 278−80.

JONES, P.: 'Saxon and Early Medieval Staines', in *Trans LAMAS* 33, 1982, 186−213.

JONES, P. E.: 'The Estates of the Corporation of London', in *Guildhall Miscellany* 7, 1956, 3−16.

JOPE, E. M.: 'Saxon Oxford and its region', in Harden, D. B. (ed.) *Dark Age Britain*, Methuen, 1956, 234−58.

KINGSFORD, C. L. (ed.): *John Stow: A survey of London*, Clarendon Press, 1971 reprint.

LOCKER, A.: 'The fish bones from Maiden Lane and Jubilee Hall', forthcoming.

LONDON: *A Chronicle of London from 1089 to 1483*, Harleian Ms 565 Cottonian Ms Julius B1, London, 1827.

MALONEY, J. and HARDING, C.: 'Dukes Place and Houndsditch: The Medieval Defences', in *The London Archaeologist* 3 No. 13, 1979, 347−54.

MARSDEN, P. R. V.: 'Archaeological Finds in the City of London', in *Trans LAMAS* 21 pt 3, 1967, 189–221.

MARSDEN, P. R. V.: *Roman London*, Thames and Hudson, 1980.

MARSDEN, P. R. V.: *The Roman Forum Site in London*, HMSO, 1987.

MEANEY, A. and HAWKES, S. C.: *Two Anglo-Saxon Cemeteries at Winnall, Winchester, Hampshire*, The Society for Medieval Archaeology Monograph Series: No. 4, 1970.

METCALF, D. M.: 'Monetary expansion and recession: interpreting the distribution patterns of seventh and eighth-century coins', in Casey, J. and Reece, R. (eds.) *Coins and the Archaeologist*, Seaby, 1988.

METCALF, D. M.: 'The Ranking of the Boroughs: Numismatic evidence from the reign of Aethelred II', in Hill, D. (ed.) *Ethelred the Unready*, British Archaeological Reports British Series 59, 1978, 159–212.

METCALF, D. M. and RIGOLD, S.: 'A revised check-list of English finds of sceattas', in Hill, D. H. and Metcalf, D. M. (eds.) *Sceattas in England and on the Continent*, British Archaeological Reports 128, 245–68.

MILLETT, M.: 'The Thames Street Section, 1974', in Hill, C. et al *The Roman Riverside Wall and Monumental Arch in London*, LAMAS Special Paper 3, 1980, 14–26.

MORTON, C. and MUNTZ, H. (eds.): *The Carmen de Hastingae Proelio*, Oxford, 1972.

OSWALD, A.: 'The Church of All Hallows, Lombard Street', in *Antiquaries Journal* XX, 510–11.

PARNELL, G.: 'Tower of London – Inmost Ward excavation 1979', in *The London Archaeologist* 4, No. 3, 1981, 69–73.

PRITCHARD, F. A.: 'Late Saxon Textiles from the City of London', in *Medieval Archaeology* 28, 1984, 46–76.

PRITCHARD, F.: 'Small Finds', in Vince, A. (ed.) *Aspects of Saxo-Norman London II: Finds and Environmental evidence*, LAMAS Special Paper 12, 1989.

RCHM Royal Commission on Historic Monuments: *Roman London*, 1928.

RAHTZ, P.: 'Buildings and rural settlement', in Wilson, D. (ed.) *The Archaeology of Anglo-Saxon England*, Methuen, 1976, 49–98 & App. A, 405–52.

RADFORD, C. A. R.: 'Excavations at Cricklade, 1948–63', in *Wiltshire Archaeological Magazine* 67, 1972, 61–111.

RANDSBORG, K.: *The Viking Age in Denmark*, Duckworth, 1980.

REDKNAP, M.: 'Little Ilford, St Mary the Virgin, 1984', in *The London Archaeologist* 5 No. 2, 1985, 31–7.

REDKNAP, M.: 'Recent work at Stratford, E15: 30 Romford Road', in *The London Archaeologist* 5 No. 11, Summer 1987, 291–6.

RICHARDSON, B.: 'Excavation Roundup 1986', in *The London Archaeologist* 5 No. 10, 1987, 270–8.

RIGOLD S.: 'The Sutton Hoo coins in the light of the contemporary background of coinage in England', in Bruce Mitford, R. L. S. (ed.) *The Sutton Hoo ship Burial* I, British Museum, 1973.

RIVIERE, S.: 'The Excavation at Mitre Street', in *Popular Archaeology* 6 No. 14, December 1985/January 1986, 37–41.

ROWSOME, P.: *Excavations at 1–6 Old Bailey (LUD 82)*, DUA Archive Report, 1984.

SAWYER, P.: *Anglo-Saxon Charters: An annotated list and bibliography*, Royal Historical Society, 1968.

SHELDON, H. L.: 'Excavations at Parnell Road and Appian Road, Old Ford E3', in *Trans LAMAS* 23, 1972, 101–47.

SHELDON, H. L. and TYERS, I.: 'Recent dendrochronological work in Southwark and its implications', in *The London Archaeologist* 4 No. 14, 1983, 355–361.

SHEPHERD, L.: 'The Saxon Church at St. Margaret's Rectory', in *Archaeology Today* 8 No. 11, 1987, 23–5.

SHOESMITH, R.: 'Excavations on and close to the defences', *Hereford City Excavations*

2, CBA Research Report 46, 1982.

STENTON, F.: 'Norman London', in Stenton, D. M. (ed.) *Essays preparatory to Anglo-Saxon England*, Oxford, 1970, 23–47.

STENTON, F.: *Anglo-Saxon England*, Cambridge University Press, 1971.

STEWART, I.: 'Anglo-Saxon gold coins', in Carson, R. A. G. and Kraay, C. M. (eds.) *Scripta Nummaria Romana: essays presented to Humphrey Sutherland*, Spink and Son, 1978.

STEWART, I.: 'The London mint and the coinage of Offa', in Blackburn, M. A. S. *Anglo-Saxon Monetary History*, Leicester University Press, 1986, 27–44.

STOTT, P.: 'Saxon and Norman coins from London', in Vince, A. (ed.) *Aspects of Saxo-Norman London II: Finds and Environmental evidence*, LAMAS Special Paper 12, 1989.

SUTHERLAND, H.: Anglo-Saxon Gold Coinage in the Light of the Crondall Hoard, Oxford University Press, 1940.

TATTON-BROWN, T.: 'The Topography of Anglo-Saxon London', in *Antiquity* LX, 1986, 21–30.

TAYLOR, H. M. and TAYLOR, J.: *Anglo-Saxon Architecture* Vol. 1, Cambridge University Press, 1965.

VCH: *The Victoria History of the Counties of England. Middlesex* 1, 1969.

VINCE, A.: 'The economic basis of Anglo-Saxon London', in Hodges, R. and Hobley, B. (eds.) 1988, 83–92.

VINCE, A. (ed.): *Aspects of Saxo-Norman London II: Finds and Environmental evidence*, LAMAS Special Paper 12, 1989.

WESTMAN, A.: 'The Church of St Alphege', in *Archaeology Today* 8 No. 11, 17–23.

WHEELER, R. E. M.: *London and the Vikings*, London Museum, 1927.

WHEELER, R. E. M.: *London and the Saxons*, London Museum, 1935.

WHITE, W. J.: *Skeletal remains from the cemetery of St Nicholas Shambles, City of London*, LAMAS Special Paper 9, 1988.

WHITELOCK, D.: *English Historical Documents* I, Eyre and Spottiswoode, 1968.

WHYTEHEAD, R. and BLACKMORE, L.: 'Excavations at Tottenham Court, 250 Euston Road, NM1', in *Trans LAMAS* 34, 1983, 73–92.

WILLIAMSON, T.: 'The Roman Countryside: Settlement and Agriculture in NW Essex', in *Britannia* XV, 1984, 225–230.

WILSON, D. (ed.): *The Archaeology of Anglo-Saxon England*, Methuen, 1976.

YORKE, B.: 'The Kingdom of the East Saxons', in *Anglo-Saxon England* 14, 1985, 1–36.

YOUNGS, S. M., CLARK, J. and BARRY, T. B.: 'Medieval Britain and Ireland in 1983', in *Medieval Archaeology* XXVIII, 203–65.

Index

Locations refer to London unless stated otherwise. Historical English county names are used throughout (ie, pre-1974). Page numbers refer to text and captions.

1300K